MW01681187

Take the Lid Off

Unleashing Your Unlimited Potential

TAKE THE LID OFF

Unleashing Your Unlimited Potential

by Carol Holm

with Cami Newsome

C&C Books
Blackfoot, Idaho

C&C Books
494 North Meridian Street
Blackfoot, Idaho
83221
Phone: 208-785-6218

www.takethelidoffbook.com

ISBN: 978-0-9840104-1-7 (hardcover)
ISBN: 978-0-9840104-2-4 (softcover)

Publisher's Cataloging-in-Publication data

Holm, Carol.
Take the lid off : unleashing your unlimited potential / by Carol Holm with Cami Newsome.
p. cm.
Includes bibliographical references and index.
ISBN 978-0-9840104-1-7 (Hardcover)
ISBN 978-0-9840104-2-4 (pbk.)
ISBN 978-0-9840104-3-1 (ebook)

1. Self-management (Psychology). 2. Self-esteem. 3. Success. 4. Performance.
5. Achievement motivation. 6. Goal (Psychology). 7. Conduct of life.
I. Newsome, Cami. II. Title.
BF697.5.S46 .H65 2011
155.2—dc22 2011938315

First Edition
Printed in the U.S.A.

DEDICATION

I dedicate this book to my family:

To my husband Dayle, who first taught me how to dream.

To my children Brett, Cami, Jason, Darin, and Ryan, and their spouses—for their willingness to support me in all of my dreams.

To my grandchildren and future great grandchildren, with the hope that the ideas in this book will give them a road map to achieve the things that are important to them, and that each will recognize their God-given potential.

TABLE OF CONTENTS

ACKNOWLEDGEMENTS

I have been working on this book for over ten years. Throughout the process, I was constantly asking for help and feedback from dozens of people, which makes it impossible to thank everyone who had a hand in its completion. But without the contribution of a few key individuals, this book would never have happened...

First of all, I want to acknowledge my daughter, Cami, who has been there every step of the way. She knows and understands the concepts as well as I do, and she was always there to listen and help me fully develop every idea. I am very appreciative of her eye for detail, inquiring mind, and patience through the years.

When we hired Joanne Smith to work in our financial advising office, we had no idea that she had a natural understanding and love for the laws of the mind, as well as the ability to put those ideas on paper. With her calm and steady personality she was there to help us past the hurdles, and to keep us moving towards our ultimate goal of having the book published.

My husband Dayle is my biggest fan. He has been such a great support to me, and even when he joined Cami and me to travel around the world, he would be there at each and every meeting, cheering me on and listening to me speak. Lately he has had to endure all of the hours I have spent working on the book, and I am grateful to him for his constant patience and love.

My friend Darren Martin was the first person to really "hold my feet to the fire" about getting the book completed and for that I am very appreciative. I also want to thank HighSpot Inc for their efforts in keeping us on the right track and helping us through the difficult process of getting a book published.

Thanks to all of my family, friends, clients, and peers, for cheering me on and having faith in me and my ability to write this book.

INTRODUCTION
Carol's Story

I have worked side by side with Carol for almost 20 years, first as her administrative assistant and now as her business partner. Someone once asked me how I would describe our relationship. My initial reaction was, "Complicated." As with any relationship there are always different dynamics, but add in the fact that Carol is also my mother and those dynamics become magnified.

Despite our differences, working with Carol has been a great opportunity. Through all the ups and downs that life brings us, she has continued to study the laws of success. I have been there to watch and support her as she tested each new piece of information that she found, to see if her latest discovery was another piece of the puzzle to achieving success.

This book could be considered a culmination of all Carol's studying and testing; I see it as the end of a long journey that began back in 1976 when she stood beside my dad, Dayle, as they watched in shock while a man from the bank locked the front doors of their failed business.

It was only three years earlier that they had eagerly opened their motorcycle and snowmobile shop, excited to have a business doing something they loved. Unfortunately, after three straight winters of record low snowfalls, they weren't selling enough snowmobiles to keep up with the mounting expenses.

At the time I couldn't tell which was more painful for them—having people stop by the house every day to collect money, or the auction that was like neon lights flashing their failure to the world. I think the final blow came as they met with an attorney who looked at the numbers and said to them, "You owe so much money, there is no way you can ever pay it all off." His solution was for them to file for bankruptcy, but neither of them felt that was the right thing to do. So instead of leaving their creditors hanging, they decided that my mom, who had been a stay-at-home mom, needed to go to work to help pay off the debt. That's how she began her career as a life insurance agent for New York Life Insurance Company.

Her first year in the business was tough; she was still devastated from going broke and now she was also struggling to manage a new career while raising myself and my three brothers. But finally, by the end of the first year, she was selling the recommended 10 life insurance policies a month.

Just when we could see things starting to improve, my parents broke the news to the family that my mom was unexpectedly pregnant with their fifth child. So there she was, desperately trying to figure out how to survive financially, but now with five young children, a struggling new career and a mountain of debt to pay off.

It was during those difficult times that her passion for studying the laws of success took on new meaning. She was like a sponge. In her spare time she was reading everything she could get her hands on. With each book she read, she kept saying that she was looking for just one new idea, one more piece of the puzzle that would help her put it all together. Each time she learned a new concept, she would experiment on herself to see if it really worked.

When I started working for Carol as her administrative assistant, I was able to witness her successes first-hand. As her passion for the laws of success grew, she found herself being asked to speak to groups of people about what she was learning. She spoke about how it was working in her life and how she applied it to her career to set and achieve goals. Soon she was sharing her ideas with audiences all across the country.

After hitting rock bottom with the closing of their business and then spending countless hours researching and experimenting, Carol decided to put together everything she had learned, and lay it on the line. She announced that she was going to be New York Life's top agent in sales.

It was at this same time that Jerry Borrowman, a trainer for New York Life who was also a published author, decided they should write a book about her experiences in the business. It would include the things she'd learned about tapping into the power of the mind. Jerry even had New York Life agree to purchase 4,000 copies of the book if she led the company in sales. The Million Dollar Round Table, a professional trade association for financial advisors, also jumped on board and agreed to publish the book if she could guarantee the sale of those 4,000 books. Talk about pressure!

In 1999 I proudly watched as Carol achieved her goal. She had become the first female in the history of New York Life to lead the company in sales, which also made her the first female to lead any major life insurance company in sales. To everyone's surprise except hers, she was number one. Carol had accomplished exactly what she said she would.

The next six weeks were a whirlwind as, together along with my Dad, we attended all the meetings for the top 4,000 agents and Carol spoke to them about how they could use the power of their mind to improve their business. Each evening after they heard her speak, a copy of her book *Have You Bought the Ticket?*[1] was delivered to their room.

At one of the meetings in Boca Raton, Florida, a company officer brought a relative who had recently lost her husband. She was a sweet middle-aged lady who was trying hard to be upbeat, but it was obvious that she was struggling with the pain of her recent loss. Following Carol's talk she came up to us and said, "After listening to you, I know I will be alright, I can do it." Somehow the ideas Carol presented to the agents about setting goals applied to this sweet lady's situation as well. The message touched her heart and gave her new hope.

It was then that I realized that Carol had discovered concepts that are not just for sales and career goals, but are universal laws that apply to everyone and every situation. Whether it's paying off debt, reaching career goals, or simply overcoming a trial in life, the concepts she's learned have proven to work in her life and mine. I also continue to hear stories of transformation from others in many walks of life about the power of Carol's teachings.

My hope for this book is that it can teach you what you need to do to reach your highest goals and ultimately live your wildest dreams. Carol's goal was to lead her company in sales, but I know her ultimate dream was to teach others about the power of the mind. In achieving her goal, she has been able to live her dream.

Cami Newsome

Carol's daughter and business partner

CHAPTER 1: The Power of the Mind

> *Man's mind, once stretched by a new idea, never regains its original dimensions.*
> —Oliver Wendell Holmes

We have all noticed people who seem to be able to achieve great things with very little effort. They seem to have it all and we find ourselves wanting the same talents, fame, or fortune that has made them so successful. We usually conclude, however, that their abilities are superior to ours and that we are incapable of achieving the same things.

> *When God made the oyster, He guaranteed his absolute economic and social security. He built the oyster a house, his shell, to shelter and protect him from his enemies. When*

hungry, the oyster simply opens his shell, and food rushes in for him. He has freedom from want.

But when God made the eagle He declared: "The blue sky is the limit, build your own house!" So the eagle built on the highest mountain. Storms threaten him every day. For food, he flies through miles of rain and snow and wind. But think of it, the eagle, not the oyster, is the emblem of America.

—AUTHOR UNKNOWN

God granted the eagle far more potential than the oyster, but God granted us unlimited potential.

Our minds are amazingly powerful; they are designed, built and ready for our use and benefit. Unfortunately, many of us either don't recognize our potential or we don't know how to take advantage of it. The key is learning how to harness the power that is already present in your mind. It's all there in one central location and when you learn to use your mind to its full potential, you release your unlimited potential.

Many internal obstacles prevent us from achieving all of our hearts' desires: a poor self-image, an inability to recognize our genius, our failure to tap into our unconscious mind, our inclination to be negative, and our fear of failure. What we have to realize is that there are also ways of thinking and acting, in accordance with the laws of success, that allow us to overcome these obstacles and achieve what we previously thought impossible. We can reprogram our self-image, discover our individual genius, and use the power of our mind, thus putting us in a position to realize our dreams.

My husband and I experienced failure and hardship first-hand when our business went under many years ago. To help us recover and get out of debt, I started a new career as a life insurance agent. To help me succeed at this job, I spent many hours reading numerous authors on the secret to success. Eventually, I came to understand the universal laws of success. I went on to apply them to my career and, as a result, became the first female to ever lead a major life insurance company in sales. In this book, I wish to share with you all that I have learned.

The fact is that we are all created equal. It's true that we each have different types of unlimited potential, talents and abilities, but we are all equipped with everything that we need to succeed. It doesn't matter what your dream is. We all have unlimited access to the resources and functions that bring success. You are the only thing standing between where you are now and what you want to achieve in the future.

I'm excited to take you on a journey of discovery, one where you learn how your mind works, your self-imposed limitations, how to correct them, and ultimately how to unleash your unlimited potential!

CHAPTER 2: Reprogramming Your Self-Image

There is a treasure deep within everyone; the adventure is to discover it.

—FROM THE MOVIE *THE LEGEND OF JOHNNY LINGO*

Almost every town in America hosts a circus each year, to the delight of both children and adults. If you've ever witnessed them setting up back when they used elephants for the task, it was amazing to observe the elephants move around the heavy pieces of equipment as they erected the large tents for the show. Once the work was done, the trainers would take the elephants to their places behind the tents, tie a rope around one of their legs, and attach the rope to a small stake in the ground. This was done to ensure that the elephants wouldn't wander away.

These massive animals were quite capable of removing a small stake from the ground, so why didn't they pull themselves free?

The reason was, when they were young, the rope tied to their leg was attached to a much larger stake driven deep into the ground. Try as they might, they would not have been able to pull it out. Eventually, they gave up trying. Once we understand this early training, we understand why elephants passively accept their fate.

Just like elephants, we have been programmed to believe that we are capable of doing certain things and incapable of others. What you think you can or cannot do is not necessarily reality. As humans, our limitations are set by our self-image[2]. It's not who we are that holds us back; it's how our minds have constructed our self-image that determines our parameters.

Your self-image is your mind's conception of the kind of person you are and what you are capable of achieving. You have created this picture from all your past experiences, including your failures and successes, as well as the way others react to you, especially in early childhood. Your conscious mind is not aware of the picture you have produced, but it is there, down to the last detail, and it controls your life.

Your self-image is the determining factor that dictates your behavior and lifestyle. It determines the type of career you choose, how you handle money, the amount of success you have, how you treat your body, and the quality of your relationships. If a person wants a healthy body, for example, but sees themselves as overweight, they will continue to struggle with their weight. If they desire a fulfilling and successful career but can't imagine anything other than frustration and poverty, they will never achieve the results they want.

Just because you believe your blueprint to be an accurate picture of who you are does not make it true. Have you ever gone to the fun house and looked at yourself in the distorted mirrors?

Some make you look tall and thin, while others cause you to appear short and fat. It's an entertaining thing to do, but you walk away knowing that what you saw in the mirrors is not a true reflection of your real appearance. Your mind often does the same thing by creating a distorted image of you that is completely wrong. If you have behavior that is self-defeating, you have a distorted self-image. Only when your self-image is in alignment with your true self do you end up with behavior that allows you to reach your full potential.

Our mind began forming our self-image while we were still in the womb. The emotions experienced by an expectant mother, be they happy, peaceful, anxious, or fearful, are also felt by the fetus. A great deal of our original programming occurs by the age of five, and much of it is complete by the time a child reaches twelve. Part of this programming comes from parents and other significant people in the child's life, such as relatives, friends, and teachers. The remaining part is a result of how the youngster was treated by society and what they were told. If at an early age a child was continually told that they were stupid, it became part of their programming. If they were told they were loved, they usually see themselves as being loveable.

A good example of how easily your self-image is molded by what you are told is provided by a school teacher named Jane Elliott. Back in 1968 she did an experiment with her students designed to help them understand what it felt like to experience discrimination.

She told them that researchers had discovered that people with blue eyes were brighter and more likely to succeed in life, and that people with brown eyes were inferior and tended to be stupid, lazy, and untrustworthy. She put arm bands on the students to distinguish which ones were superior and which ones were inferior. Students who had previously been best friends became enemies. The superior students started being cruel and disrespectful to their inferior classmates. The brown-eyed students became cowardly, allowing the blue-eyed students to treat them badly. Their school work also began to decline rapidly, as they struggled to complete even simple assignments.

After the experiment continued for a few days, the teacher made the announcement that there had been a mistake. It was actually the brown-eyed students who were superior and the blue-eyed students who were inferior. The results quickly reversed. The test scores of the brown-eyed students became far superior to the scores of the blue-eyed students. The new superior group began treating the new inferior group in the same cruel manner that they had been treated.

There was a lot of controversy over this experiment and it would never be allowed in the schools today. But it proved how easily the self-image can be programmed and reprogrammed, and how quickly it can happen when the mind believes what it is being told. It also proves that mistakes can happen if someone gives you inaccurate information about your potential.

The problem with our early programming is that we were too young to have any input on its accuracy. Our original programming will always be with us; it's not like a bad computer program that can be thrown away and replaced with a better one. The stronger the emotion with which we acquired our programming, the stronger the hold it will have on us. However, as we mature in judgment, it becomes our responsibility to determine the accuracy of the information we receive. We also have the ability, through our thoughts and choices, to create a new self-image that is capable of overriding the original one. In other words, we have the power to reprogram our self-image.

This power is illustrated in a 1913 novel by Harry Leon Wilson titled *Bunker Bean*. It is an intriguing story about how an insecure, timid man was tricked into believing in himself. Bunker Bean's mother was an extremely judgmental woman, constantly criticizing everything he did and turning her son into a nervous, timid creature. When Bunker was just a child, his mother died, and his ineffectual father remarried. Bunker went to stay with his relatives in the big city where, even during his time at college, he continued to live timidly through his terrors. He felt he was inferior to others and he was afraid of everything, including himself. He was even afraid of policemen "whom he never passed without a tremor."

Bunker's first employer was an old man who was writing a book on reincarnation. As they worked, Bunker learned of "karmic cycles" and "the astral plane." He began to wonder if he too had lived before; if his present state of being "was a reward or a penance." Sometime later, during a particularly low ebb in his affairs, Bunker saw a newspaper ad showcasing Countess Casanova—Clairvoyant—Answers the Unasked Question. And so Bunker visited the countess and wrote upon her magic slate: "Who was I in my last incarnation." A misspelled answer soon appeared: "The last time you was Napolon Bonopart."

Bunker Bean was shocked to learn that people had once been in awe of him. How could Napoleon have been so courageous, while Bunker Bean was so timid and fearful? He bought biographies to read and a print of the crowning of the Emperor. He was determined to regain all of the qualities he once possessed. He spent hours dreaming about past victories and tried to incorporate the thinking of a great man into his own life. His confidence improved and he began to look people in the eye. It didn't matter that associates still thought of him as the old Bunker Bean, for he now knew the truth about himself. But the more he read of Napoleon's character and career, the more he came to dislike the rough "Corsican upstart."

He returned to Countess Casanova, wanting to know about the earlier, more benevolent bodies he'd inhabited. The countess and her companion, Professor Balthasar, told him that he'd been an Egyptian ruler: the tall, handsome, wise and beloved King Ram-tah. That same day, Bunker finally received the $10,000 inheritance that had been held in trust since his mother's death. He immediately gave half of it to Balthasar so that he could search out and eventually purchase King Ram-tah's mummy.

The new-found confidence saw Bunker "expand his chest, draw in his waist and stand erect." He began to speak up for himself, to become witty and at times masterful, to make new friends and even to court the boss's daughter. And when a business cabal tried to buy his company shares for well below their projected value, he bested them by buying yet more of those shares, netting himself $400,000 on the deal.

Then one day he discovered the precious mummy Balthasar had purchased for him was a papier-mâché fake and all the wonderful things he had been told about his former lives were not true. He realized that he had never been a king or a spectacular leader, just Bunker Bean all along. "He had become once more insignificant. Forever now he must be afraid of policemen and all earthly powers."

But when Bunker visited Paris and stood among the glories of Napoleon's tomb, he also realized that upstarts were men who believed in themselves, and that he had become someone through such a belief. He had learned a great truth: that to believe is all that matters. "Be upstart enough and all things are yours." He knew that Bunker Bean, the lowly, had "the power to magnetize, to charm, to affront the world and yet evoke monuments—if he could only believe it."

I was lucky to have grown up in a loving family where I felt accepted and cherished. I was a bubbly, happy child, and my parents called me their "sunshine girl." To this day you will seldom see me without a smile on my face. There was, however, one particular quirk in my original programming. I often heard my parents say, "Don't get too big for your britches." Continually hearing this and other negative comments about success created a natural fear of striving to succeed. My basic instinct became to sabotage anything that would lead to visible success.

When my daughter, Cami, first came to work as my administrative assistant she noticed my tendency to do this. I was like the person driving down the road with one foot on the gas pedal and the other on the brake. I would do everything right to succeed. Then, without knowing, I would sabotage my efforts, making my chances of success very difficult. After Cami brought this to my attention, I thought about what I was doing and realized that she was right. In order to help me get past this problem, she started hiding the reports and kept me busy focusing on my goals, so I didn't have time to think about the results in terms of success. This strategy worked short term. For long-term success, however, I had to go back to my mind and reprogram my self-image.

I started by making a list of reasons why I shouldn't succeed and a list of reasons why I should. I ended up with only three reasons not to succeed and thirty-one reasons to succeed. The answer became obvious to me: my reasons to be successful well outweighed any of the reasons why I shouldn't. It was then that I realized it was time to reprogram my self-image and to stop viewing success as an enemy. I have made a lot of headway in reprogramming my mind toward success, despite occasional setbacks. When I notice my behavior slipping back to its old ways, I remind myself that it is okay to be the person I am capable of being and not the person I thought I should be.

So how do you go about reprogramming? Although you may have had very little control over your original programming, you have complete control over the two areas that have the greatest impact on the ongoing direction of your self-image: your thoughts and your actions. These thoughts and actions, in turn, are determined by your habits. One study says that up to 90 percent of our everyday behavior is based on habit. So if you were to change your habits, your self-image will automatically change. And when you change your self-image, your habits will change to match. As soon as you begin a new habit, good or bad, you begin the process of changing your thoughts and actions, which will then reprogram your self-image.

Changing your thoughts and your actions begins when you decide to take responsibility for your choices. The result is that you end up with behavior that is congruent with who you really are. "Reprogramming Your Self-Image" is therefore a process of moving into alignment with your true self.

So if our habits determine our self-image, how do we change our habits to develop the self-image we want? Start by choosing only one habit to work on at a time. It takes energy and focus to begin the process of change.

For example, picture yourself learning how to juggle. There is a step-by-step process you go through. First you master throwing one ball in the air and catching it. Next you add a second ball until it becomes natural. You then add a third ball and practice until you are adept at handling all three balls at the same time. The key to juggling is only adding one ball at a time and practicing until it is no longer difficult. If you tried learning to juggle starting with four balls, you would probably get frustrated, give up, and never develop the skill.

It works the same way when it comes to changing habits. As humans, we are not designed to change more than one habit at a time. If you are trying to change too many habits at once, it becomes easy to get frustrated, give up, and never change. Think about New Year's resolutions. They seldom work because people try to change too many habits at the same time. They start out with great resolve, making several resolutions and two weeks later they give up and wait until next year to do the same thing. The truly destructive element is that each time they do this they are adding negative programming to their self-image. They are teaching themselves to believe that they can't be trusted to follow through on things they've started.

When you work on only one habit at a time, you are being as efficient as possible. Once it becomes a habit, it will no longer take the same amount of energy and focus to continue the desired behavior. Most experts say it takes twenty-one days to change a habit. My experiences have taught me that it can take more or less time depending on how willing a person is to accept it as part of their new self-image. I recommend that you make a list of habits that you want to acquire and then pick one to work on each month. If you find that after a month it has not become a habit yet, continue working on it during the next month.

The following are some examples of habits you could work on:

- Exercise regularly
- Get 7 to 8 hours of sleep each night
- Smile
- Be on time
- Make a budget and stick to it
- Schedule quality time each week for your family
- Change negative thoughts to positive thoughts

A good indicator that you have made a habit part of your self-image is when it becomes uncomfortable not to do it. Reversing the new habit would take more energy than just doing it. It's at this point that you can switch your focus and start working on a new habit, just like a juggler adds another ball.

When you make positive changes in your habits, it creates a paradigm shift in your mind. This shift doesn't come from a desire to see yourself differently; it comes as you become acquainted with the real you.

As mentioned earlier, up to 90 percent of everything you do during the day is done from habit, so you can almost picture your mind as a computer program. It can only do whatever you have programmed it to do, and it can only produce information based on your input. If you make a mistake inputting data, the computer will give back inaccurate information. But if you input the right data, the results will be correct.

Just like a programmer works to correctly and accurately program a computer, you are the programmer for your self-image. This means that you are the only one with the power to program your mind. Others may influence your decisions, but they have no power to input the data.

I was once told a story about a boy named Monty who was the son of an itinerant horse-trainer. When Monty was a senior in high school, his teacher gave the class the assignment to write about what they each wanted to do when they grew up. Monty wrote that he wanted to own a ranch and train horses, and he drew a detailed diagram of the property, the large ranch-house and the out-buildings. His teacher gave him an F and explained that the grade reflected that he deemed Monty's dream unrealistic. No boy without money or resources would ever be able to buy a ranch, purchase breeding stock, and pay the necessary stud fees. When he offered Monty the chance of rewriting his paper for a higher grade, Monty told him, "You keep the F and I'll keep my dream." Today Monty Roberts owns a 154-acre horse-training facility in the Santa Ynez Valley, in California.

Monty didn't let the negative message from his teacher have an adverse impact on his self-image. He ignored the message and stayed true to himself. He was in control of what was being programmed.

There are many habits that can have an impact when it comes to reprogramming our self-image. Some examples include choosing to eat better or get into shape, becoming debt free or sticking to a budget, working on relationships with others, or becoming a more valuable employee. Along with developing life-changing habits there are four activities that will directly influence your self-image.

1. Write a description of your desired self-image and read it daily.

A man is what he thinks about all day long.
—Ralph Waldo Emerson

First of all, you need a blueprint of who you want to be. I have found that one of the most effective ways to do this is to sit down and write out your desired self-image. You could write a detailed paragraph, make a list, include pictures—it doesn't matter what the format, as long as it helps you to imagine the person you want to be. Reading your description daily will help program your new self-image into your mind.

Another useful tool in changing how we see ourselves is self-hypnosis, which can also be referred to as meditation. During the hypnotic stage we tap into the teachable part of our brain where our self-image was originally formed. Once we are in this relaxed state, we have far more power over programming our mind.

The following are the six steps that you can follow for self-hypnosis:

1. Sit in a comfortable, quiet place. Find a location where you are not easily disturbed or distracted.
2. Take a deep breath, as deep as you can, and very slowly exhale. Repeat the deep breath and slowly exhale three times. With each breath in, feel your chest and belly rise, and imagine breathing in peace and calmness. With each breath out, feel your chest and belly relax, and blow out all the tension or anything else getting in the way of relaxing. By this time you'll notice a calm come over you.
3. Begin relaxing by tightly squeezing the muscles in your body and letting them relax. Start with your feet, move

to the calves in your legs, and continue up the rest of your body.

4. After your whole body feels relaxed, imagine yourself at the top of an escalator. Step on the escalator and ride down, slowly counting backwards from twenty. By the time you reach the bottom, you should be very relaxed.
5. Enjoy the tranquility for several moments. While you are in this hypnotic state, begin to experience yourself as you want to be—remember, it's not who you currently are, but who you want to be. Try visualizing an upcoming event and see it vividly in your mind. See yourself handle the situation exactly the way you want. You can also picture something you want to accomplish and imagine your desired outcome in all its detail.
6. Now go back on the escalator and ride up. Count to ten. When you get to ten, open your eyes, feel relaxed, refreshed, and wide awake.

Develop the habit of spending at least 20 minutes a day on this refueling, life-changing exercise. You'll be amazed at the results.

2. Always say things to yourself about yourself that you want to be true.

You probably don't realize it, but every time you say something to yourself about yourself, you are programming your self-image. It's what **you** say to yourself, not what **others** say to you, that programs your mind.

Always ask yourself if what you are saying is really what you want as part of your programming. Something as simple as saying that you have a poor memory will cause you to have a less effective memory. Many people complain that they are unlucky.

When they do that, they are programming their self-image to make sure they are unlucky. If you want to be lucky, tell yourself that you are lucky. If you want to be happy, tell yourself that you are happy and, if you want to be rich, tell yourself that you are rich. When you continue to say these things, your mind eventually believes you and acts accordingly.

Your mind is never blank. You spend a great deal of time each day talking to yourself and most of these conversations are about you. Start focusing on self-talk that improves your self-image. As you do this you will notice that positive feelings follow. Feelings match thoughts. And since you are in control of your thoughts, you are in control of your feelings. Whenever you feel bad, it is an indication you are thinking negative thoughts. When you make a habit of surrounding yourself with a positive environment, it makes it easier to have positive feelings.

We all have times when we allow ourselves to have negative thoughts. Have a game plan for shifting your thoughts, such as listening to uplifting music, going for a walk, or talking to a good friend. Try spending 30 days saying only things to yourself about yourself that you want to be true. You will find that you have a more positive self-image.

3. Attach a positive meaning to each event that occurs to you.

Along with telling ourselves things that damage us, we can also make mistakes in how we attach meaning to the events in our lives. Each time something happens, we go to our mental database, which acts like a filing cabinet in our mind, storing all our memories and knowledge. It searches through all the files to find a past experience that is similar to what just happened. Based on its findings, the mind attaches a meaning to the incident and assumes that it is correct. This system is often flawed and we sometimes attach a meaning that is completely inaccurate. Most disagreements are caused by people attaching an inaccurate meaning to an event.

For example, if you are shopping in the grocery store and see a friend who fails to say "Hi" or wave hello, your first impulse is to think that they are being rude or they are mad at you. This assumption can lead to hurt feelings and possibly holding a grudge when maybe the truth is that they were simply in a hurry and didn't see you.

The event + your response = the outcome
(The formula is E + R = O)

You can't change the event, but you can change your response and that will change the outcome.

This formula can also be applied to situations that are beyond your ability to control. In 1998 Michael J. Fox stunned the world by announcing that he had been diagnosed with Parkinson's disease, a degenerative neurological condition. In his book *Lucky Man*[3] he says: "Before Parkinson's, when so much of my identity was tied up in my acting career, the question that burned inside me was, 'How long can I keep living like this?'" After the diagnosis he decided to choose a life that centered on the thing that was most important to him, his family. His quote on the back cover of the book says: "The ten years since my diagnosis have been the best ten years of my life, and I consider myself a lucky man." For many people, being diagnosed with Parkinson's would be a devastating blow to their self-image and yet Michael chose to remain positive.

4. Choose books, movies, music, TV shows, and friends that have a positive impact on your self-image.

Most of us would not choose to go to a dumpster and rummage for food to put into our bodies, yet many people choose to fill their minds with a constant barrage of garbage.

What you choose to consistently expose yourself to, you will eventually incorporate into your life. Books, music, movies, and even people, all have an energy level that is either positive or negative. For example, listening to music with a positive energy level raises your own energy level. The same applies to the people in our lives. They say you become like the five people you spend the most time with. Also, when you read about people like Abraham Lincoln, Mother Teresa and Gandhi, you will find yourself taking on some of their qualities. If you are constantly exposed to stories about people with an unhealthy lifestyle, don't be surprised if you begin to exhibit that same behavior in your own life.

To emphasize again; whatever we choose to expose ourselves to, we will eventually incorporate into our lives. Every book you read, every movie you watch, every song you listen to, and every person you spend time with has an impact on programming your self-image—good or bad.

Sometimes the thought of reprogramming your self-image may seem overwhelming. Some of you have suffered from traumatic experiences that have been difficult to move past. I had the opportunity to hear Dave Pelzer speak at a meeting a few years ago and to feel his sweet, forgiving spirit. Dave wrote a book titled *A Child Called "It"*[4] chronicling his childhood. He suffered one of the most gruesome cases of child abuse in California's history. Dave's mother was mentally ill and an alcoholic. For some reason, out of five young boys, she chose Dave to abuse. It's hard to describe the abuse he suffered from his own mother but it included starvation, torture, humiliation and alienation. Dave's father was aware that Dave was being abused, but he turned his head to what was going on and finally abandoned him by moving out.

Miraculously Dave survived and was eventually placed in foster care. What is more amazing is that Dave somehow found the support and developed the skills so he could live a normal, happy, productive life. Dave eventually discovered his father in a hospital, dying of cancer, and was able to finally forgive him. He is a role model for anyone who has suffered abuse and wants to move past it. He is also a role model for all of us who want to reprogram our self-image.

One of the greatest discoveries of the 20th century was the exploration of our self-image. Perhaps one of the most powerful ideas of the 21st century is our power to reprogram our self-image.

CHAPTER 3: Your Individual Genius

> *A winner is someone who recognizes his God-given talents, works his tail off to develop them into skills, and uses these skills to accomplish his goals.*
>
> —Larry Bird

Every human being has potential genius in at least one area. This potential is created at a very early age. Shortly after you were conceived, you began developing brain cells called neurons. Before you were even born, these neurons began communicating with each other through connections called synapses. By the age of three your brain had created trillions of synapses. But, as fast as you created these connections you began losing them by the process of elimination, which is commonly referred to as "synaptic pruning." The connections that were frequently used remained strong and intact, while those used less frequently became weak and eventually went away. By your mid-teens, half of your original connections were lost. However, the remaining connections became your potential abilities and talents.

Throughout the remainder of your life, this network of stronger and weaker connections will not change by very much. Your brain will still continue to produce synapse connections from learning and having different experiences, but these connections don't significantly alter your original basic network of stronger and weaker connections. They simply add dimension and strength to your existing network.

Through this process of weeding out the weaker synapses, your individual strengths became hardwired into your system. This, combined with genetics, is why art comes easily to one person, while another will love math, and still another will be good at anything mechanical.

Imagine there is a meadow. In that meadow there is a duck, a fish, an eagle, an owl, a squirrel, and a rabbit. They decide they want to have a school so they can be smart, just like people.

With the help of some grown-up animals, they come up with a curriculum they believe will make a well-rounded animal:

running,
swimming,
tree climbing,
jumping,
and flying.

On the first day of school, little br'er rabbit combed his ears, and he went hopping off to his running class.

There he was a star. He ran to the top of the hill and back as fast as he could go, and, oh, did it feel good. He said to himself, "I can't believe it. At school, I get to do what I do best."

The instructor said, "Rabbit, you really have talent for running. You have great muscles in your rear legs. With some training, you will get more out of every hop."

The rabbit said, "I love school. I get to do what I like to do and get to learn to do it better."

The next class was swimming. When the rabbit smelled the chlorine, he said, "Wait, wait! Rabbits don't like to swim."

The instructor said, "Well, you may not like it now, but five years from now you'll know it was a good thing for you."

In the tree-climbing class, a tree trunk was set at a 30-degree angle so all the animals had a chance to succeed. The little rabbit tried so hard he hurt his leg.

In jumping class, the rabbit got along just fine; in flying class, he had a problem. So the teacher gave him a psychological test and discovered he belonged in remedial flying.

In remedial flying class, the rabbit had to practice jumping off a cliff. They told him if he'd just work hard enough, he could succeed.

The next morning, he went on to swimming class. The instructor said, "Today we jump in the water."

"Wait, wait. I talked to my parents about swimming. They didn't learn to swim. We don't like to get wet. I'd like to drop this course."

The instructor said, "You can't drop it. The drop-and-add period is over. At this point you have a choice: either you jump in or you flunk."

The rabbit jumped in. He panicked! He went down once. He went down twice.

Bubbles came up. The instructor saw he was drowning and pulled him out. The other animals had never seen anything quite as funny as this wet rabbit who looked more like a rat without a tail, and so they chirped, and jumped, and barked, and laughed at the rabbit. The rabbit was more humiliated than he had ever been in his life. He wanted desperately to get out of class that day. He was glad when it was over.

He thought that he would head home, that is parents would understand and help him. When he arrived, he said to his parents, "I don't like school. I just want to be free."

"If the rabbits are going to get ahead, you have to get a diploma," replied the parents.

The rabbit said, "I don't want a diploma."

The parents said, "You're going to get a diploma whether you want one or not."

They argued, and finally the parents made the rabbit go to bed. In the morning the rabbit headed off to school with a slow hop. Then he remembered that the principal had said that any time he had a problem to remember that the counselor's door is always open.

When he arrived at school, he hopped up in the chair by the counselor and said, "I don't like school."

And the counselor said, "Mmmm, tell me about it."

And the rabbit did.

The counselor said, "Rabbit, I hear you. I hear you saying you don't like school because you don't like swimming. I think I have diagnosed that correctly. Rabbit, I tell you what we'll do.

You're doing just fine in running. I don't know why you need to work on running. What you need to work on is swimming. I'll arrange it so you don't have to go to running anymore, and you can have two periods of swimming."

When the rabbit heard that, he just threw up!

As the rabbit hopped out of the counselor's office, he looked up and saw his old friend the Wise Old Owl, who cocked his head and said, "Br'er rabbit, life doesn't have to be that way. We could have schools and businesses where people are allowed to concentrate on what they do well."

Br'er rabbit was inspired. He thought when he graduated, he would start a business where the rabbits would do nothing but run, the squirrels could just climb trees, and fish could just swim. As he disappeared into the meadow, he sighed softly to himself and said, "Oh, what a great place that would be."[5]

As this story shows, the problem with genius is that it doesn't feel special to the person who possesses it. It comes so naturally that it's easy to take for granted. Without realizing, you simply assume that anyone can do it as easily as you can. That is not true. No one else in the whole world can perform things in your area of genius the way you do. Take, for instance, Muhammad Ali. He scored a low 78 on an army IQ test, yet he was a genius at boxing and promoting himself. Muhammad didn't focus on his weaknesses; he focused on his strengths.

There is a book written by Catherine Nomura and Julia Waller with Shannon Waller titled *Unique Ability®: Creating the Life You Want*[6], in which they describe four levels of competency in activities.

Incompetent Activities: These are activities that make you feel frustrated and stressed because you're just not good at them. You may have put a lot of effort into these, but you still don't get a good result. You may find yourself in conflict with others when you're doing these things because of your low skill level. Everything in this area feels difficult and makes you feel like a failure.

An example of one of my incompetent activities is filling out paperwork—I have no patience for the process, which means unless I really focus, I can easily miss important details. To make up for this, I ensure that I hire staff that have great skill at this and I rely on their talents to fill out paperwork.

Competent Activities: There are other activities that you are merely adequate at. You do fine, but others could do them much better than you. When you are engaged in these activities you feel anxiety and competition because you worry about falling behind or being replaced. These activities are boring to you and your efforts seldom pay off because there is little improvement in your performance over time.

When I began working at New York Life there was another agent who started at the same time. He succeeded as an agent, but he was only average. He soon realized that being in sales did not tap into his genius and so he decided to become a trainer. It didn't take long for him to become one of the most sought-after trainers in the industry. He is a genius when it comes to remembering data and turning complex ideas and rules into simple solutions.

Excellent Activities: These are activities in which you have superior skill and reputation, but you have no true passion for. In fact, you may not even like to do them. Others, however, like to work with you in this area because your abilities meet the highest standards.

My friends' daughter was a young struggling artist who was going back to school to complete her education. She needed a math class for her generals and called her dad to tell him that she had signed up for Calculus 2. He tried to talk her out of it, explaining that she hadn't even taken Calculus 1 yet. She took Calculus 2 anyway and ended up with the highest score in the class for the semester. Her teacher tried to get her to change her major to take advantage of her knack for math, but she explained that, even though it came easy to her, she simply had no passion for it.

Unique Ability® Activities: These are activities for which you have superior abilities and a great passion. You love doing them and they create more energy than they use up. In fact, when you are engaged in these, you lose track of time! If such an activity is part of your job, you would still do it even if you didn't get paid for it. If you have had any training in this area, you were probably the star student because you've got natural ability. These are areas of your life where you find yourself constantly improving. Think of any professional athlete. They have a superior skill that turned into a profession. Yet you can almost be guaranteed that, even if they weren't playing professionally, they would still have a passion for the activity.

In our society we have always been taught to work on our areas of weakness. However, time spent working on your area of genius will result in a much more efficient use of time and is far more rewarding. It also does wonders for your self-image and allows you to bring more benefit to society. Also, most people think "genius" has to do with IQ. The problem with the IQ test is that it only measures intelligence in academic terms. That is why doing poorly in school is little indication of one's ability to succeed in life. A person's genius may be in an area that doesn't show up in the class room.

The following are some ideas to help you recognize your areas of potential individual genius:

- Spend time thinking about what you want your life to be like. Your individual genius is tied to your purpose in life and you will feel drawn to it.
- Ask people who know you well what they think your individual genius is.
- Listen for compliments. You will find the compliments you receive have a theme to them and this theme is centered on your potential genius.
- You will have a natural passion for your genius. Think back to your childhood. What did you have a passion for?
- Learning in your area of genius will come naturally and will make sense to you. Which subjects in school did you excel in?
- You will feel more satisfaction while doing it. Become aware of which activities in your life bring you the greatest joy. Which activities rejuvenate and energize you?

Remember to allow yourself to spend time in the areas you have a passion for. If you enjoy painting, schedule more time in your life for this activity. If you enjoy being around people, there is a reason for it, so structure your life accordingly. You will find that once you discover and develop whatever it is that you are passionate about, your self-image will also improve.

Learning to spend time on your areas of natural strengths will give you far greater results for the time spent. This concept is consistent with the Pareto Principle, or "the 80/20 Rule" Pareto's Law states that a small fraction of effort accounts for the greatest amount of results. This means that 80 percent of the value of your work comes from only 20 percent of the activities you do. When you spend the majority of your time doing activities that match your genius, your positive results go up dramatically.

Although psychologists have conceived of many ways to classify personality traits, I have found Personalysis®[7] to be one of the most effective instruments to identify your individual traits.

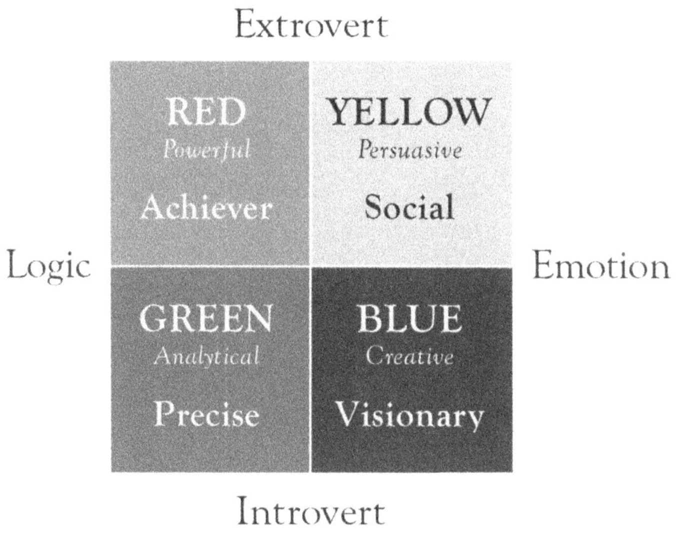

The following chart describes four basic groups of personalities:

RED and YELLOW *people are* ***Extroverts***
They are energized by interacting with people and being active
They need people and activities to recharge their batteries

GREEN and BLUE *people are* ***Introverts***
They are energized when they have time to be alone
They recharge their batteries from within

RED and GREEN *people respond with* ***Logic***
They base their decisions primarily on facts and figures
They are action oriented

YELLOW and BLUE *people respond with* ***Emotion***
They base their decisions primarily on trust and intuition
They are people and thought oriented

RED: Accomplish things by taking charge and working hard
YELLOW: Use their influence to create team work to get things done
GREEN: Precise and detailed in accomplishing their objectives
BLUE: Creative in finding new and better ways to do things

No category of traits is better than another. Each have their strengths and they each have their weaknesses. Some people will have one dominant trait, which makes them easy to predict because they almost always act the same way. But most of us have one dominant color and then at least one other color that also influences how we act. This means we will act one way part of the time and then suddenly shift to a different behavior.

Learning what color combinations individuals around you have can help you to recognize the reason why they react in a certain way to different situations.

RED: *Leader and achiever*

People with a strong tendency for the RED trait love a challenge and need to achieve. They are natural leaders, therefore business owners and leaders of companies often have a great deal of RED. Their focus is not on people, it's on getting things accomplished. That's why their social skills are sometimes lacking. They often view vacations and interactions with people as something that gets in the way of what they really want to do—which is work. These are the people whose courage and drive have helped make America what it is today.

If this is your dominant trait, be aware that you value work over people, and you may offend others.

YELLOW: *Social and persuasive*

Those with strong yellow traits generally have great people skills and are often found in sales and politics. Since they enjoy being around people, they are the peacemakers who want everyone to get along. This group usually has a broad array of careers to choose from because they can be so adaptable and charming.

Life seems to come easy for YELLOWs because of their charisma. Therefore they often take it for granted and forget to put in the effort necessary for success. Hopefully they have some RED or GREEN along with their YELLOW or they will have a lot of fun but never get anything done. If they can develop good work habits to go along with their natural people skills they can do almost anything they want to do.

GREEN: *Analytical and precise*

GREEN people are good with details and will make sure things are done accurately. Engineers, accountants, and computer programmers almost always have a lot of GREEN. The GREEN person wants very little social interaction and in fact usually feels awkward in social settings. Even though they may not have outstanding people skills they are often the most sought-after employees when it comes to administrative assistants. You simply can't train a person to have an eye for detail. They either have it or they don't.

If you score high in this category and low in YELLOW and BLUE you probably come across as stiff and hard to get to know. Be sure to choose a career that takes advantage of your attention to detail.

BLUE: *Artistic and creative*

You'll find actors, musicians, artists and beauticians in this category. BLUE is perhaps the most loveable of all the traits but also one of the most vulnerable. BLUE people just want to be loved and to make everyone's surrounding more beautiful. They are also visionary, and can see the potential for the future in a way that none of the other traits can. This is the trait that often has the hardest time finding a career that matches their genius because their talents tend to be specialized. People with this trait sometimes get caught in a fantasy world and never learn to support themselves.

If you have BLUE, make sure to take advantage of your creativity, your vision, and your eye for beauty.

It's important to remember that when you combine two colors such as RED and BLUE you don't end up with purple. I'm a combination of RED and YELLOW, which means that sometimes I am focused and driven and other times I am very social and outgoing. In the office I am mostly RED, but occasionally my YELLOW will come out; my staff often jokes about the two contrasting sides of Carol. When I'm RED, everything is intense and I want to get things done right away. In this state it is not uncommon for me to walk away and get back to work while the rest of the office is gathered together and socializing. On the other hand, when I'm YELLOW I'll sit down and chat, often interrupting everyone else from what they are trying to accomplish. There was this one time when we had a terrible storm, resulting in downed trees and the power being knocked out. The schools were being closed and even businesses and city offices were shutting their doors. I was so focused on what needed to be done that I was oblivious to the storm. I was still trying to figure out what we could accomplish with no lights and no computers. Finally Cami had to pull me out of my focused state to convince me that we needed to close the office and send everyone home.

When you look at Cami's colors you will see the exact opposite of me because she is GREEN and BLUE. This color combination makes her very stable and grounded. Having a great deal of GREEN means that Cami pays attention to the details, so fittingly she is the one in charge of our finances. At the same time her BLUE, creative side made it natural for her to design and decorate when we built a new office building a few years ago. When people walk into our office they almost always comment about the serene feeling it creates. The office is a reflection of the same stable, calm feeling Cami's personality tends to create with our staff and clients.

When it comes to our daily interactions with other people, we have frequently been taught to follow The Golden Rule: "Do unto others as you would have others do unto you." This rule is great when it comes to honesty and courtesy. However, it can be counter-productive when we consider that each category wants something completely different from each other.

RED: *need to be respected for their accomplishments*
YELLOW: *need to be liked by others*
GREEN: *need to feel secure and in control*
BLUE: *need to feel an emotional response*

Humans are very complex and no two people are alike, so these are generalities that may help make some sense out of people's behavior based on their color grouping. Keep in mind that there are hundreds of tests that look at how we behave from different points of view. This is just one of the many facets of our personality.

Once you have discovered and understand your own personality traits, it's then easier to determine your potential unique genius. But in order to use them to reach your full potential, you must be willing to develop your talents and abilities. In Malcolm Gladwell's book *Outliers*[8] he teaches us what great musicians and athletes and those successful in any field have in common. They each spend hours and hours perfecting their talent. In fact, Gladwell states that it takes about 10,000 hours of perfect practice to turn your talent into genius. Dan Sullivan in his *Strategic*

Coach® program teaches that it takes about 10 years to develop our genius. This equals about 10,000 hours.

I can still remember a Sunday evening on February 9, 1964, when Dayle and I gathered around his parents' television set. Our family, along with 73 million other Americans, anxiously awaited the first appearance of the Beatles on *The Ed Sullivan Show*. Their popularity stormed America in a way that no other singing group had ever done before and has probably never been matched since. Yet most of us had no idea what it took for this group to be prepared for the opportunity that had come their way. Earlier in their career they had been a small-time rock band performing a one-hour gig once a week or so in Liverpool. Then they were invited to play in Hamburg, Germany where they played seven nights a week for eight hours a night and were thus forced to improvise, develop new material, and perform across all genres. By the time they came to America they had already spent well over 10,000 hours developing their genius.

You probably know that Bill Gates was the math whiz who dropped out of Harvard to start a little company called Microsoft. What most people don't know is that he joined a computer club as an eighth grader and spent the next five years of high school obsessively working on computers to develop his programming skills. By the time he dropped out of Harvard at the end of his sophomore year, he had already amassed a great deal more than 10,000 hours. Developing his talent not only changed Bill's life, but the results of his talents have had a revolutionary impact on the computer industry.

As you can see, developing your genius doesn't happen overnight. Talents require time and practice to develop. This might be one of the reasons why very few individuals develop their individual genius, but when they do they always stand out and are an inspiration to others. Develop the habit of looking for the genius in everyone you meet. When you learn to recognize genius in others, it will become easier to see it in yourself. Also, as you rub shoulders with other people's genius, you learn from them and become better in those areas yourself. One word of caution however: never compare yourself to someone else in their area of genius.

As you turn your potential abilities into "Your Individual Genius" you will begin to have intuitive breakthroughs that could serve yourself, your family, your business or maybe even the world. The great inventions, art, music, and literature we enjoy today came from intuitive breakthroughs by people who have developed their individual genius.

CHAPTER 4: Your Goal-Seeking Device

> *"You" are not a machine. But new discoveries in the science of Cybernetics all point to the conclusion that your physical brain and nervous system make up a servo-mechanism which "You" use, and which operates very much like an electronic computer, and a mechanical goal-seeking device.*
>
> —Maxwell Maltz, *Psycho-Cybernetics*

In addition to a self-image and individual genius, the human mind has another power that most of us are unaware of—the power to achieve the goals we set. This power resides in your unconscious mind and is called the "Goal-Seeking Device."[9] It is the conscious mind that sets a goal, but it is the vast database of the unconscious mind that helps us attain it. The conscious mind may be the boss, but the unconscious mind does most of the work.

Imagine an outfielder in a baseball game who wants to catch a pop fly ball. The conscious mind has only one thought: to catch the ball. To accomplish this, the outfielder has to determine how fast the ball is traveling, how high it will go, and where to put his mitt to catch the ball. It is his unconscious mind that makes all the calculations to ensure the mitt is in just the right position at the right time to catch the ball.

When the outfielder was a young boy playing catch with his father, he probably dropped the ball a lot. His conscious was telling him to catch the ball, but his unconscious didn't have enough practice to put all the data together to actually do it. With practice and time, however, his unconscious figured out all the necessary calculations. The trained outfielder therefore only has to relax, not let his conscious mind interfere, and trust that his unconscious mind will get the job done.

Michael J. Gelb in his book *How to Think like Leonardo da Vinci*[10] states: "Neuroscientists estimate that your unconscious database outweighs the conscious on an order exceeding ten million to one. This database is the source of your creative potential. In other words, a part of you is much smarter than you are. The wisest people regularly consult that smarter part."

Although it is not dimensionally accurate, the following illustration can help you visualize the massive amount of data we have available for our use.

Databases of the Unconscious and Conscious Mind

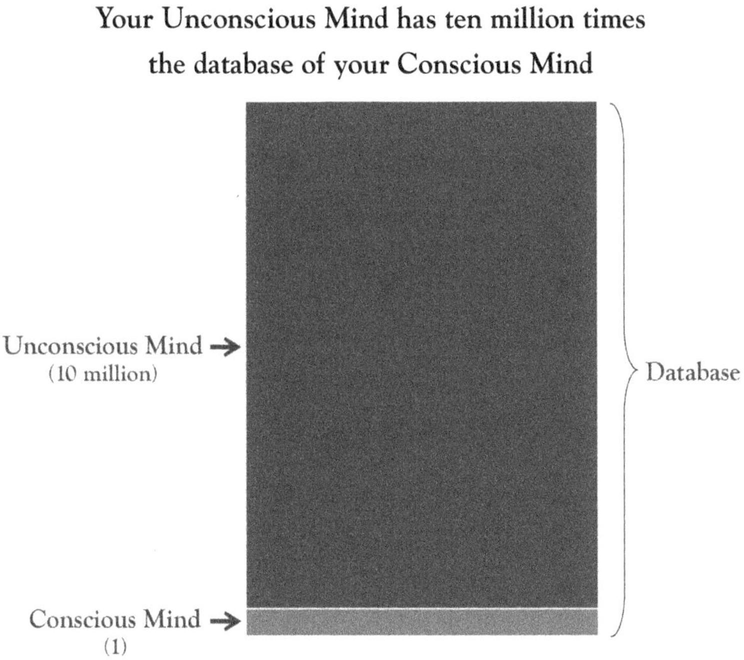

The problem is that the conscious mind can often inhibit the natural power of the unconscious mind. The following descriptions show how each part of the mind works:

Your Conscious Mind

- Decides what the goal is
- Makes the decision to develop the necessary skills and habits to achieve the goal
- Often interferes with the process by confusing your unconscious mind with criticism and fear

Your Unconscious Mind

- Achieves the learning and habits
- Uses your knowledge, senses, nerves, and muscles to accomplish the goal

- Does most of the work and, in return, asks only for your conscious mind to stop making its job so hard

You would have noticed the interplay between the conscious and unconscious mind if you ever learned to play an instrument, like the piano. At first the conscious mind must focus on placing the fingers on the right keys. However, once the pianist learns the music, they must relax and trust their fingers to play the melody without conscious thought. At that point, if they try to focus on what keys their fingers should hit, the melody will be choppy and stiff. They must relax and trust their goal-seeking device to do the job so the music can flow freely.

We can often see the battle between the conscious and unconscious mind in sports as well. When athletes get tense, they have shifted their thinking from their unconscious mind to their conscious mind. They attempt to play with willpower instead of trusting their instincts. When they are able to relax when the pressure is on, they trust their goal-seeking device to pull off the big play.

Most people do not realize that they have memory cells, not only in their brain, but throughout their entire body. It is the muscle memory that resides throughout our body that allows us to become proficient in any activity. This explains why learning to ride a bike becomes a lifetime skill we never forget. Whenever we practice something, we augment memory; the more we practice the better we get. Once we have that memory in place, we can relax and trust our goal-seeking device to carry out the actions much better than we can do with our conscious effort.

Your goal-seeking device is involved in everything you do. It accomplishes even simple actions, such as reaching for an object. When a decision is made to pick something up, the message goes to the stored data in your unconscious mind to determine how to accomplish the task. When you drive to work each morning, you usually go the same way. When you get there you probably don't even remember the trip. That's because your goal-seeking device took over.

Your Goal-Seeking Device:

- Is a built-in automatic guidance system
- Carries out your goals, once your goal is defined by your conscious mind
- Functions from data stored in your memory (including synthetic memory)
- Works behind the scenes
- Is on the job 24 hours a day, 7 days a week
- Functions only in the present and cannot function in the future or the past
- You cannot direct the operation, you can only define the goal
- Fails to function properly during moments of self-consciousness, depression, grief, distress or when you lack self-confidence

Your goal-seeking device functions much like a guided missile. A guided missile has a section called the guidance system that directs the missile and calculates the most effective path to the target. The guided missile doesn't go in a straight line, but zigs and zags as it continually corrects its course. Your goal-seeking device also zigs and zags in search of the most efficient path to its destination.

Another way to look at your goal-seeking device is to compare it to using a GPS navigation system. Once you input your destination, it tells you step by step how to get where you want to go. If you make a wrong turn, the system will tell you a new road or route to get back on track. Your goal-seeking device also searches for solutions and opportunities that help you reach your goals. When it comes to doing any activity, it doesn't tell you what to do, but actually takes over and completes the task if you can relax and trust it.

Your goal-seeking device is a function of your unconscious mind and, as amazing as the unconscious mind is, it can work for you or it can work against you. In other words, your goal-seeking device can function as a success mechanism or a failure mechanism.

Most of us know a friend or family member who constantly states "if it weren't for bad luck, I wouldn't have any luck at all." Little do they know when they say this, they are actually instructing their goal-seeking device to function as a failure mechanism. They are telling their goal-seeking device that their goal is to have "bad luck" and so it simply does what it's told.

Be aware that if we allow ourselves to, we can harm ourselves in many other ways. For example, reports indicate that a large percentage of all illnesses are caused by negative thinking, constant worry, and the pursuit of unrealistic perfection or stress. Once you understand how easily influenced your mind can be, you realize how important it is to choose positive thoughts.

The control center for your goal-seeking device is your Reticular Activating System (RAS). Each time you set a goal, you send a message to your RAS to focus on anything that will help you achieve it.

The Reticular Formation is a mass of millions of nerve fibres and neurons, about the size and shape of your little finger, located inside the brainstem. It connects with major nerves in the spinal column and brain, and works together with the RAS and its millions of communication pathways that run to and from the brain and body.

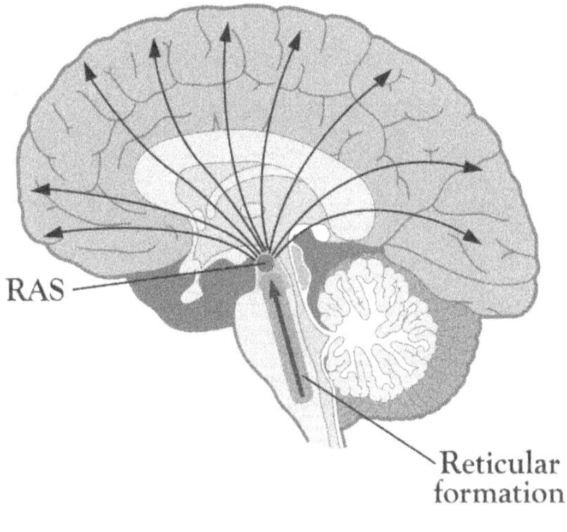

At any given moment there are as many as 100 million bits of internal and environmental information streaming into your brain. It is the job of your RAS to receive all incoming data and scan and prioritize that data, all the while taking into account your self-image (your values, beliefs, and needs). Your RAS acts like a vigilant administrative assistant who screens visitors, phone calls, and e-mails, forwarding them to the sensory and motor systems, allowing only the important ones to get through to each boss.

Once your RAS determines what's important to your self-image, it then deflects the trivial and allows only the vital information through to alert your mind. Without the RAS, your mind would be bombarded with more information than it would know what to do with causing you to flounder with all the confusion.

Have you ever noticed that when you decide to buy a new car suddenly you see the very same make and model every time you turn around? Cars similar to yours were just as plentiful prior to your purchase, but now you have told your RAS that particular car is important to you. So it allows any data related to that car to filter through to your awareness.

When you set a goal you are instructing your RAS to focus on anything that will help you achieve it. Doing this causes your mind to be on the lookout for opportunities and information that it would normally miss or filter out if you hadn't set the goal.

The RAS is the control center for your goal-seeking device, but your self-image is the gate keeper that determines how your RAS will filter the information. If you set a goal that is not consistent with your self-image, your RAS will either miss the opportunities and those ideas will never be transferred to your mind, **or**, your RAS will send the message but your mind will reject it, thinking it isn't relevant.

When you don't set goals you miss all of the potential information that could make your life better because it never makes it through the filters.

All you have to do is know where you're going.

The answers will come to you of their own accord, and at the right time.

—Earl Nightingale

How the RAS Works

- You have to set a goal. When you don't set a goal, your RAS has no project to work on.
- Trivial information is filtered out and is not allowed through into your awareness
- If you set a goal that doesn't match your self-image, your RAS sees helpful information as irrelevant and doesn't allow it into your awareness
- When you set a goal that matches your self-image, your RAS looks for solutions, and those solutions are allowed into your awareness

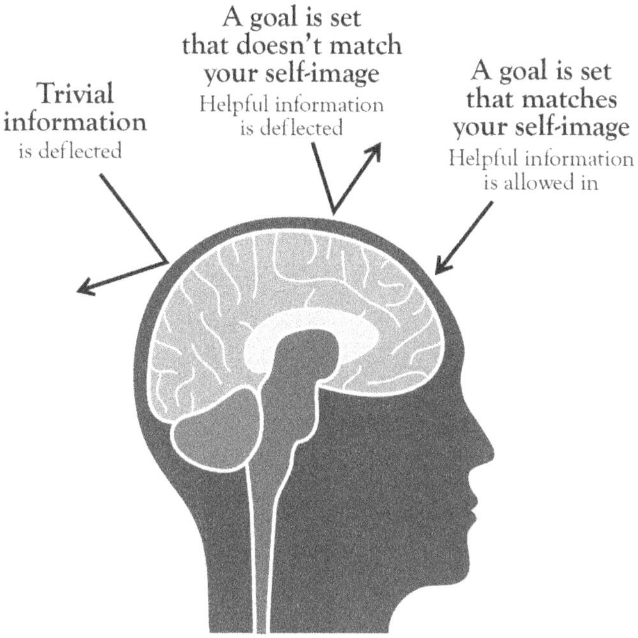

Once you set a goal, your massive database and its unlimited awareness are on the hunt for solutions, and you will think of things that hadn't occurred to you before. You'll wake up in the morning with new thoughts and solutions. Throughout the day an idea will pop into your head. You may decide to take a class, read a book, or talk to someone who has done what you want to accomplish. By simply setting a goal, you release an army of helpers with one thing in mind: accomplishing your goal.

> *The intellect has little to do on the road to discovery. There comes a leap of consciousness, call it intuition or what you will, and the solution comes to you, and you don't know how and why.*
>
> —Albert Einstein

During one of our industry meetings, Randy Marshall, who once played baseball for the Kansas City Royals, shared the following story with us. Randy's son, John, played baseball for his high school team and one day he announced he was going to hit his very first home run for his father's 50th birthday. Randy repeatedly told his son he didn't have to hit a home run, all he expected was for him to do his best. Just like all parents, he didn't want his son to set such a high goal and then be disappointed if it didn't happen.

Finally the anticipated birthday arrived and John was up to bat. Sure enough, he hit the ball and it went sailing over the fence for a home run. He was up to bat two more times and each time he hit the ball, it went out of the park. John not only hit his first home run for his fathers' birthday, he hit three home runs that day. Randy proudly related the story to us, complete with videos of each of the three home runs and shots of Randy enthusiastically cheering from the sidelines. He also showed us clips of the story that went on to be highlighted on the local news broadcast.

How could a young man hit three home runs in one game when he had never hit a home run before in his life? John didn't understand how the goal-seeking device worked; he simply set a goal, practiced until he was prepared, and then had faith it would happen. You don't need to understand how your goal-seeking device works either, as long as you have enough faith in the goal-setting process to put it to work.

When you don't set goals, you waste the amazing power of your goal-seeking device. When you set too many goals at one time, your RAS gets confused about which one to focus on.

CHAPTER 5: The 32 to 1 Rule

When dealing with people, let us remember we are not dealing with creatures of logic. We are dealing with creatures of emotion, creatures bustling with prejudices and motivated by pride and vanity.
—Dale Carnegie

Every January millions of people decide to get in shape. They start out with great resolve to begin eating healthily and exercising regularly. They are excited as they visualize the results and positive impact it will have on their lives. Two weeks later they've given up on their goals and they're back to their old habits.

Why do we get excited about our goals and then sabotage ourselves when it actually comes down to making it happen?

Your mind is constantly on the lookout for you; it wants you to experience pleasure and avoid pain. How many times have you found that what you *want* to do is far more influential on your decisions than what you *think* you *should* be doing? The logical mind knows the facts and thus assumes it knows what is best for you, yet the emotional mind functions from feelings and has a stronger pull for what you want to do. So the problem is this: when it comes to setting goals, most are created by the logical mind. You choose a goal based on what you *know* you *should* be doing. However, your emotional mind tends to get in the way because most goals take some level of sacrifice and hard work, and your emotional mind keeps telling you that you want to avoid anything that may cause you pain.

The challenge is to overcome the tug-of-war between your logical and emotional mind. You need to get the power of your emotional mind on board with what your logical mind wants.

The 16th century humanist Erasmus of Rotterdam once wrote in his essay "The Praise of Folly" that the ratio of reason to passion is "half an ounce to a pound." Although he was writing satirically, this statement helped to illustrate a concept to me that I had always known was true. When you calculate half an ounce to a pound the ratio becomes 32 to 1. Realistically there is no way to prove the ratio of emotions to logic is a definitive 32 to 1; perhaps it could be as large as 100 to 1, or as little as 3 to 1. It will even be different from person to person and situation to situation. Despite the fact the ratio has no basis in science, I know from experience that emotions exert a greater influence on our decisions and overall goal achievement than logic.

To keep things simple and for illustrative purposes, I have decided to call this theory the "32 to 1 Rule." Although not dimensionally accurate, the correlation would look something like this:

Your Emotional Mind is 32 times more powerful than your Logical Mind

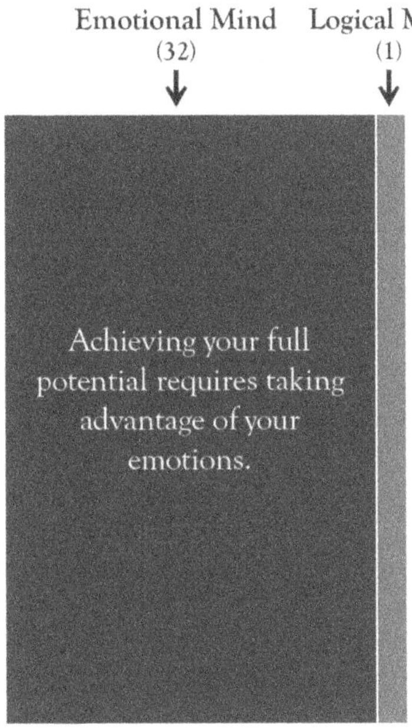

Neuroscientists have proved that the brain relies on emotion over intellect in decision making. This means that most of our decisions are based on our desire to feel good. We can be persuaded by reason, but we usually react based on emotions and then justify our actions with logic.

Take for example last year when I decided to trade in my car. The make of car I was driving consistently had problems and I had to take it out of town to get it repaired. However, despite the constant repairs, I loved driving that car. As I began my search for a new one, the dealership I was working with showed me a chart which proved that the make of car I was driving had a history of needing more repairs than average. My logical mind knew I should buy a different make of car with a better history of maintenance, but I ended up buying the exact same make that I had been driving. Instead of buying a car that I logically thought I should, I bought the one I wanted because I loved the way it looked and how it handled.

Although your emotions determine most of your decisions, there are things that you can do to get your emotions to work with your logical mind when it comes to the goal-setting process.

1. Develop the right habits.

> *The common denominator of success—the secret of every man who has ever been successful—lies in the fact that he formed the habit of doing things that failures don't like to do.*
> —ALBERT E. N. GRAY, *THE COMMON DENOMINATOR OF SUCCESS*

The habits you develop not only create your self-image; they also determine what you will and won't do in any set of circumstances. Your mind is designed to be efficient, and habits make that possible because habits override your emotions. For instance, once you develop the routine of exercising regularly, you no longer think about the pain. In fact it feels uncomfortable to miss a workout session.

If you are in sales and you have developed the habit of making calls every day, you will make calls without stopping to think about the possible rejection.

While you are in the process of developing new habits, don't tempt your emotions. If you love chocolate cake and you're on a diet, don't keep chocolate cake around. Your logical mind wants to lose weight, but your emotional mind wants to eat some chocolate cake. Since your emotional mind makes the majority of the decisions, your willpower will probably buckle and you will eat the cake. Once it becomes a habit to choose healthy food, you can have chocolate cake around and you are much less likely to eat it.

Keep in mind the earlier suggestion of working on only one habit at a time. Until something becomes a habit, you are fighting your emotions' desire to feel good. Once something becomes a habit, you would be fighting your emotions if you stop doing it.

If you want to get in shape, start with one habit and then move to the next. Don't ever try to do them all at once because your emotions will get in your way. They will convince you that the whole idea of getting in shape is simply not worth it. Win your emotions over one habit at a time.

2. Measure your activities and report the results.

The TV series *The Biggest Loser* is a popular reality show that tracks the results of people who want to lose weight. It's exciting to watch contestants succeed at something they have struggled with most of their lives. Once they join the show they have a high probability of success because the odds are in their favor. First, they have trainers who teach them how to eat so they can reduce the amount of calories they consume. Second, the trainers teach them how to increase the calories they burn by ramping up their exercise with a rigorous workout regimen. These trainers also work closely with each participant every day and cheer them on as they begin to change lifelong habits. Finally, the participants must weigh in each week and be accountable for their progress on national television. It is their accountability in front of millions of people, along with the habits they have formed, that almost guarantees their success.

When you report your activities, your odds of success go up exponentially. Reporting can be either a painful or rewarding experience, depending upon the results. Most people would rather put up with the pain of dieting and exercise in order to avoid the pain of having bad results when they report. The more respect you have for the person you are reporting to, the more pressure you will feel and the higher the odds that you will succeed.

When I was a new life insurance agent we were required to attend a weekly sales training meeting. At the end of each meeting we would take turns going to the blackboard and posting how many calls we made and how many appointments we held, along with our number of sales. After three years I was no longer required to attend those meetings and my results quit improving.

Years later I decided it was time to start being accountable again. I had continued to keep track of my activities, but now I began sending a report of my activities each month for an entire calendar year to someone I admired. Each year I would choose a new person to send my reports to and the report went out every month even when I hadn't met my objectives.

One particular time I chose a former manager who had moved to St. Louis. In March of that year I decided to stretch my thinking, so I set a huge goal for April that was way beyond anything I had ever done before. At the bottom of my report to Danny I disclosed my goal. On April 10, Danny called to ask how I was doing and I proudly answered that I had accomplished 20 percent of my goal. He responded with, "Well then, you're only 80 percent short." I started to stammer when he said, "It's okay Carol, I know you can do it" and hung up. I walked into Cami's office, told her what happened and stated, "When I put that on my report I didn't really mean I was going to accomplish that much in one month. I was just trying to push myself to set higher goals." I was expecting Cami to sympathize with me, but instead she simply said, "Well, we better work harder and make the goal then!" With no excuses left, I increased my efforts and did 117 percent of my goal that month.

For years I have spoken about the power of setting goals and reporting results at meetings for our industry and invariably someone from the audience has asked if they could send their reports to me. Several times I have agreed to do this and the pattern has always been the same. They would start sending their reports, but then they would have a bad month and pretty soon the reports stopped. Being accountable is a difficult thing to do. In order to make this work we have to be willing to let our weaknesses show and most of us hate to be that vulnerable. So be aware that if you decide to be accountable you will also have times when you don't measure up to your expectations.

Marshall Goldsmith in his book *Mojo* talks about how he enlists the help of his friend Jim in achieving his personal goals. Every day, no matter where they are in the world, they try to connect on the phone so they can ask each other a series of questions. They're important day-to-day lifestyle questions, such as, "Did you say or do anything nice for your wife?" "How much do you weigh?" or, "How many minutes did you write?"

After 18 months of adhering to this ritual, Jim and Marshall both weighed exactly what they wanted to weigh, exercised more, and got more accomplished. As an experiment, they decided to quit for a year to see what would happen. Each of them put the weight back on and didn't accomplish nearly as much.

If you have what it takes to put your ego on the line and report to someone, you have what it takes to complete your goals. Having to report not reaching a goal is often more painful than any pain associated with sacrificing in order to achieve your objective.

3. Add passion to your goals

The standard method of goal-setting is what I call Traditional Goal-Setting (explained in greater detail later in the book). This is used to achieve the day-to-day tasks and logical goals that are required of us. Since these tasks are usually mundane and repetitive, we hardly ever put additional effort into achieving them. Occasionally we even find ourselves becoming neglectful or lazy. The key then becomes finding a way to add passion to the desire of achieving these goals. A strong emotional connection to your goals will make it easier to meet and even exceed them.

Take for instance a person who decides to lose weight because their doctor recommends it. It is an important goal, but most people have a hard time staying motivated because it takes dull, daily tasks, such as eating right and exercising regularly, to achieve it. If that same person had a high school reunion coming up that they had decided to attend, they are more likely to lose the weight. That's because they would be motivated by emotion, the desire to look good when they see their former classmates.

Adding emotion to goal-setting is one of the easiest and most effective ways to help us achieve our goals. In my early career I found myself working to just pay the bills. I realized it was time to push myself to do better, so Dayle and I decided that I would set a much higher sales goal. If I reached it, we would take our family to Disneyland for the first time.

The emotion I added was the desire to give my family the fun experience of visiting Disneyland. I made a chart on a poster board with my goal at the top and 12 markers along the way to keep track of my monthly progress. We held a family meeting and showed our children pictures of Disneyland, and showed them the chart, and said that I was going to report to them how I was doing every week.

Doing business was easier that year because I was motivated by a higher purpose than simply earning an income. Each night when I got home our children were waiting for me at the door to find out how my day went. When I came home early they wanted to know why I wasn't still working. At the end of the year I achieved my goal and our family enjoyed a fantastic vacation.

There are so many ways to add emotion to your goals. Try a number of different methods until you find the one that works best for you.

CHAPTER 6: The Law of Attraction

> *You are a living magnet. You invariably attract into your life the people, circumstances and resources that are in harmony with your dominant thoughts, especially those thoughts magnetized by the power of emotion, either positive or negative.*
> —Brian Tracy

While enhancing your self-image and tapping into your individual genius and unconscious mind are crucial in attaining your goals, another key to achieving success is to utilize the Law of Attraction. The Law of Attraction holds that "like attracts like." More specifically, you attract into your life the results of the thoughts you dwell upon and what you feel you deserve.

Each of us acts like a magnet; we attract conditions that are in accord with our thoughts and energy.

Magnets have both positive and negative poles; they either attract objects or repel them away. Just like the magnet, we can attract what we want or we can repel it away. If a person sets goals to be financially successful but continually has thoughts of hardships and struggles, they will repel the very success they desire and instead attract hardship and struggles. On the other hand, if we develop the habit of focusing on our goals and have faith they will happen, eventually we will achieve success.

The Law of Attraction functions in our lives on three different levels. Our thoughts impact our mind and our relationships with others, and they reach out into the world and attract back to us the results of our dominant thoughts.

Our Thoughts Impact Our Mind

A couple of years ago my granddaughter read a book about the Law of Attraction and she excitedly said to me, "I just learned that it is not what we eat that makes us fat, it's what we think that makes us fat."

As powerful as our thoughts are, they can rarely override the other laws of nature and of our society. You may believe you can jump out of a 10-story building without getting hurt, but the law of gravity will take over and cause your body to hurl to the ground. When it comes to our weight, if we consume more calories than we use up, we will gain weight. You may want to be President of the United States starting tomorrow, but the laws and governmental procedures of the United States inhibit that from happening.

Even though our thoughts can rarely override any of the other laws of nature, we can learn to work with them. For instance, before 1903, a manned, heavier-than-air flight was only a dream.

When it comes to our weight, the law of self-image simply states that we will always behave in a way that is consistent with the image we have of our self. In other words, we create what we unconsciously think we deserve. If our dominant thought is that we are always at our ideal weight and develop the habits that are consistent with maintaining our ideal weight, then our thoughts can make us thin. When people struggle with their weight they usually do just the opposite by obsessively thinking, "I don't want to be fat." If that is their dominant thought, they will unconsciously choose habits that cause them to be overweight.

As you can see, the Law of Attraction doesn't distinguish between what we want and what we don't want. It merely attracts into our lives what we think about. When we think, "I don't want to be poor" it registers in our mind as, "I want to be poor" and then it proceeds to bring that into our lives. Try changing your self-talk to something that matches what you want, such as, "I'm hard-working and I manage my money well."

Our Thoughts Impact Our Relationships with Others

Studying Ohm's acoustic law teaches us more about the Law of Attraction. Take two tuning forks with the same physical characteristics and hold them close together. If you strike one of the forks causing it to ring, the non-ringing fork will begin to ring as they resonate with each other. People can also resonate with each other when they share common frequencies. It is our energy level that determines our frequency which in turn determines with whom we choose to associate and the quality of our relationships.

Dayle and I have five children and some of them have Attention Deficit Hyperactivity Disorder (ADHD) and dyslexia.

As you can imagine, dealing with their behavior in the school system was a challenge. My focus was: "I don't want to have problems with my children." But the Law of Attraction translated this as: "I want to have problems with my children."

During one of our more challenging times, a friend called to tell me about an upcoming seminar in our area. The seminar was designed to help a person become more emotionally healthy. When she first asked me to go with her, I told her I wouldn't be able to attend because I had a conflict that evening. Suddenly I found myself saying that I would change my schedule and go. As a result, Dayle and I and our five children attended the seminar. As we entered the two-day seminar, I had one goal in mind, and that was to change our children's behavior.

It was a miracle. Seven people went into the seminar and emerged two days later a completely different family. You may ask, did the children stop swinging from the chandeliers? The answer is no, they were still hyperactive. Did they start doing better in school? Again the answer is no; they were still dealing with learning disabilities. So what happened in those two days that made such a difference? The only thing that changed was me and my thinking. I quit stressing about how I wanted things to be different with my family and started appreciating the special people they were. Yes, they are very active, but they are also thoughtful and a lot of fun to be around. I started loving each one of them unconditionally and I quit worrying about what other people thought. I even stopped attending parent-teacher conferences until I was strong enough to not let it affect my relationship with my children. I changed my thinking and in turn it had a positive impact on our whole family. Remember the formula: Experience + Response = Outcome (E + R = O).

The following story illustrates how our thoughts impact our relationships with others.

A man pulled into a gas station on the outskirts of town. As he filled his tank, he remarked to the attendant, "I've just accepted a job in town. I've never been to this part of the country. What are people like here?" "What are the people like where you came from?" the attendant asked? "Not so nice," the man replied. "In fact, they can be quite rude." The attendant shook his head. "Well, I'm afraid you'll find the people in this town to be the same way."

Just then another car pulled into the station. "Excuse me," the driver called out. "I'm just moving to this area. Is it nice here?" "Was it nice where you came from?" the attendant inquired. "Oh yes! I came from a great place. The people were friendly and I hated to leave." "Well, you'll find the same to be true of this town."

Our thinking creates the type of relationships we have. If you are struggling with a relationship, check your thoughts. Start focusing on the strengths of others and you will be amazed at the results.

Our Thoughts Go Out Into the World and Attract the Results Back to Us

Our inner thoughts are projected outward into the world around us and like a magnet we attract the conditions that match our thoughts.

Picture how television works, with each station broadcasting on a different frequency. If you want to watch channel 8 you must tune to the proper frequency to pick up that channel. When you change channels, you change frequencies.

Just like the different channels, every thought we have goes out into the universe on a frequency that matches our thoughts. It then connects with like frequencies and attracts into our lives people and situations that match our frequency. When you set a goal and believe that you will achieve it, all the sudden people and situations will come to you to help you reach that goal.

We have all experienced this law but perhaps didn't know what it was. The time you were thinking about someone and then out of the blue they called and said: "You've been on my mind so I thought I'd call." When you set a goal and things happen to help you reach your goal yet you can't explain how they happened, it's probably the law of attraction functioning in your life.

For several years I had the goal to be a speaker on the Main Platform at the Million Dollar Round Table. This was a goal I didn't have control over and therefore the results would have had to come from a source outside of myself.

The Million Dollar Round Table is a worldwide organization for financial advisors. Each year approximately 31,500 members from around the world are invited to attend a four-day meeting, with about 6,000 choosing to attend.

Each morning during the three-day meeting, they have a Main Platform where all 6,000 attendees can enjoy a power-filled experience. During this portion of the meeting the attendees have the opportunity to listen to speakers and performers that have included Christopher Reeve; Dave Pelzer, who wrote *A Child Called It*; Frank Abagnale, author of *Catch Me If You Can*[11]; and

The Mormon Tabernacle Choir. One year they even had a circus. In addition to the professional performers, they choose three or four financial advisors from their membership to speak. As you can see, the odds of being chosen to speak on the main platform are long.

Because the goal was on my list, I went to Chicago several times to take a speaking class. I also accepted the opportunity to speak every chance I got so I would be prepared when the opportunity came. I also told myself twice a day for several years: "I'm a speaker on the Main Platform at The Million Dollar Round Table."

Amazingly, because I put it out there, in 2000 I spoke on the Main Platform in San Francisco! I spoke in between Bill Porter (whose story inspired the movie *Door to Door*) and The God Squad (a priest-rabbi duo who had a weekly TV show and newspaper column). I spoke again in 2006 on the Main Platform at the MDRT's Experience Meeting in Thailand.

When you set goals and have a belief that they will happen, even if the results are largely outside of your control, something magical occurs. If you have experienced this phenomenon, you know what it feels like.

When you have faith in yourself and your goal, amazing things just happen. If one opportunity falls through, another one comes along to take its place. You don't need to concern yourself with the failures along the way because they will not affect the final outcome. All you have to do is make a plan, do everything you can, and have faith that your goal-seeking device will find the opportunities and the law of attraction will attract the solutions you need. You will reach your goal and you won't have a clue how it happened.

Choosing positive thoughts strengthens your belief in yourself and others. That in turn increases your positive thoughts, causing more people and situations to come to you for your good, and the cycle continues to get stronger and stronger.

On the other hand, negative thoughts create fear and worry and you begin to doubt yourself. When you worry, your negative thoughts attract the very things you fear into your life, causing your own negative situations.

Positive Cycle

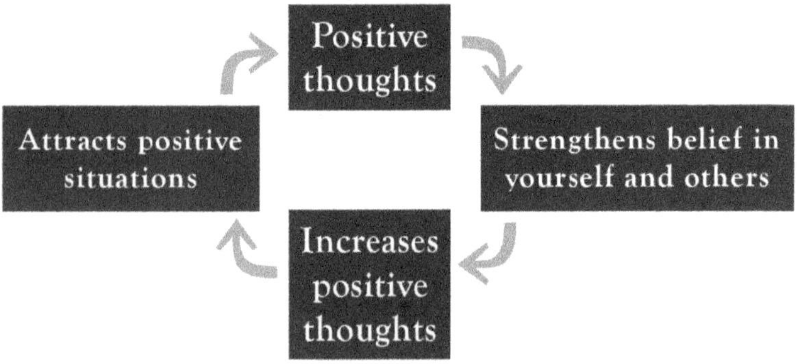

Negative Cycle

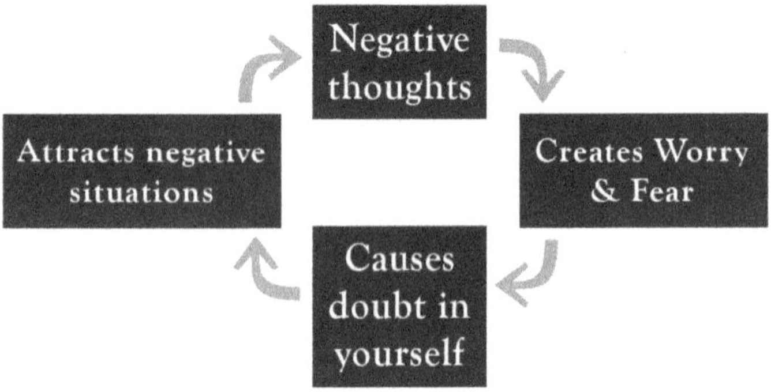

If you have just lost your job and your thoughts are optimistic, those thoughts will be projected out into the world. If your dominant thought is fear and panic, you will attract those results into your life as well. When things go wrong, it is natural to begin to doubt yourself, so you must have a plan to change your thinking to positive when this happens.

Once a person understands this law it is easy to become concerned about the negative thoughts that so easily creep into your mind. Don't become obsessed with stopping these thoughts. It will only make it worse. Remember earlier in the chapter when I explained that if you tell your mind "Don't," it registers as "Do"? Instead, each time a negative thought pops into your mind, replace it with a positive thought. If you work on this until it becomes a habit, you will find yourself doing it without conscious effort.

CHAPTER 7: Synthetic Experiences

If one advances confidently in the direction of his dreams, and endeavors to live the life which he has imagined, he will meet with a success unexpected in common hours.
—HENRY DAVID THOREAU

When it comes to bridging the gap between your self-image and your goal, a great technique is to create a synthetic experience, which is an imagined state of affairs. While we know it is not true, our goal-seeking unconscious does not, and it will cause the Law of Attraction to work as if it were.

There are two different forms of imagination:

Synthetic Imagination takes advantage of the existing data in your mind from your experiences, education, and observations, and creates something entirely new and different. This type of imagination allows you to rearrange the data you already have available into a completely different form, thus allowing you to come up with entirely new concepts.

Creative Imagination taps into the intelligence in space and allows you access to information that has not yet been introduced to your mind. It is as though you are able to plug into a gigantic computer of knowledge and ideas. Geniuses in any field tap into this power in order to take them to a level that is incomprehensible to the ordinary man.

Nothing has ever been created without first being seen in the mind of the creator. Imagination created the airplane, the computer and the Empire State Building. It is impossible to accomplish anything without first seeing it in your mind. When your mind sees a great idea and you believe that you can bring it to pass, at that point, it is already done. Use your imagination to look at your future and picture it any way you want it to be.

To show you the power of your own imagination, imagine you are holding a lemon in your hand. Roll it around and feel its texture. It feels slightly cool and waxy. Picture yourself putting the lemon on the cutting board, picking up a knife and then slicing it in half. As you cut it, small drops of juice roll down the side. You pick up one of the halves, tilt your head back and squeeze the juice into your mouth. Feel your mouth start to water and your body shiver as it reacts to the taste of the tart juice.

If you were able to vividly imagine tasting the lemon juice, your body physically reacted to something that only happened in your mind—something you created out of your imagination.

The field of medicine has been aware of the impact of placebos for years, and lately they are doing more experiments to determine how much impact our thinking has on our ability to heal. The placebo effect is accomplished by giving a patient a sugar pill and telling them it is medicine designed to make them better. In many cases, the sugar pill has the same positive effect as the real pill would have had.

There are three different strategies that take advantage of your imagination and the fact that your unconscious mind doesn't know the difference between a real and a vividly imagined experience.

1. Self-Affirmations

These are directives, stating in present tense with plenty of descriptive words what you want to have happen.

For example, if you want to buy a new home, you wouldn't say: "I am going to buy a home." You would state: "I live in a beautiful new home in the country." Or maybe: "I live in a high-rise condo by the beach in Boca Raton."

The reason I suggest that you state it in the present tense with plenty of descriptions is that your unconscious mind responds to the language of emotion, not logic. Picture yourself visiting Paris and trying to speak English to someone who only speaks French. They won't understand you. It works the same way with your mind. If you try to tell your unconscious mind what you want it to do by using logical language and directives, it won't respond because it can't understand you, and so the results will never happen. By stating your affirmation the way I have instructed, you program your self-image to believe that you already own the home, therefore it gives the okay to proceed and your goal-seeking device permission to start the process. When you add plenty of descriptive words you add emotion, and it also gives your goal-seeking device more information to work with. Reading: "I live in a high-rise condo by the beach in Boca Raton" creates far more emotion than: "I am going to buy a home."

2. The "Act As If" Principle

This is an effective way to choose whatever behavior you want to have. Simply begin acting as if you already have the desired behavior and before long it will become a natural way of behaving for you.

If you want to be happy, act happy. Smile, stand up straight, and put a chipper sound in your voice, and then think of things that make you happy. It is not the events in your life that determine whether or not you are happy. Being happy is a choice.

On the other hand, being unhappy is also a choice. If you want to be unhappy, act unhappy. Get a whiny tone to your voice, and slump your shoulders. Then think of all the rotten things that have ever happened in your life. If you do this often enough, it will become a habit.

For several years my husband Dayle and I helped teach the Dale Carnegie course as graduate assistants. There was a chant we learned that I still say to myself every morning before I get out of bed. It goes like this:

Act enthusiastic and you'll be enthusiastic.
Act enthusiastic and you'll be enthusiastic.
Act enthusiastic and you'll be enthusiastic.
Boy, am I enthusiastic!
—Author Unknown

When I first began my career as a life insurance agent, even though I worked very hard, I had little success at selling insurance policies. However, when someone would ask how I was doing, I would always optimistically state that I was doing great! In reality I *was* doing great because I was making a lot of phone calls. I knew that eventually my hard work would pay off. So when you are in a situation that you feel unsure about, act confident and you will be confident.

Another example is the story of Frank Bettger, who played baseball for a minor league team in Pennsylvania. Frank had always thought he was doing a good job until one day he was fired. He asked the manager why, and was told that he was lazy, that he trotted around the bases like a tired and worn-out vet. Frank said he hid his nervousness and fear by seeming nonchalant and the manager advised him to wake up and put some enthusiasm into his next job. Playing in New Haven, Connecticut, he was the most enthusiastic player on the field. Soon the newspapers were reporting that he was like a ball of fire creating an enthusiasm for his team that was contagious. Eventually, he was chosen to play for the St. Louis Cardinals. After an injury cut short his career, Frank went on to sell life insurance and wrote the popular book *How I Raised Myself from Failure to Success in Selling.*[12] Frank incorporated the "Act As If" Principle.

If you want to be thoughtful, act thoughtful. If you want to be forgiving, act forgiving. If you want to be successful in your career, act if you are already successful.

3. Visualization

In December, 1960, the *Research Quarterly of the American Association for Health, Physical Education and Recreation*[13] reported on an experiment with basketball players that examined the power of synthetic experiences. Professor L. V. Clark of Wayne State University divided 144 Detroit high-school students into two groups, with each group holding varsity, junior and novice players. Both groups were taught a new shooting technique. The first group was told to practice the technique each morning for two weeks. The second group was instructed to only mentally practice the new technique.

At the end of two weeks, the varsity and junior kids in both groups, whether practicing physically or only mentally, improved at almost the same rate. Only the novice students showed a much greater improvement with physical practice.

The experiment showed that practicing in our mind is almost as effective as physically practicing. Even though that experiment was done many years ago, the results remain valid and visualization is still used today by most professional athletes. They have found that if athletes can see it in their mind, they can bring it to pass in reality.

One method is to picture that you are in a movie theatre watching yourself on the big screen. If you play basketball, see yourself dribbling down the court straight to the basket and dunking the ball.

Another more common method is to visualize your situation from within. Instead of watching yourself on a screen you would observe the situation the same way you would if you were actually having the experience. If you are bowling you would see your arm deliver the ball as it goes down the alley for a strike.

If you want to get out of debt, see a zero balance on your statements. If you want to save $2,000,000, see your statement showing a savings balance of $2,000,000. Every time you look at your statements, see the desired numbers in your mind.

Regardless of the method you use, the impact on your mind will be strengthened when you include as many of your senses as possible. What sounds can you hear, what do you smell, and what do you see?

If you are giving a speech, visualize the audience listening attentively as you focus on the passion you feel about sharing your message. Too often we do just the opposite, as we visualize ourselves failing and looking like an idiot.

The story of Roger Bannister, who in 1954 was the first person to run a mile in under four minutes, summarizes perfectly the power of visualization. The world record had stood at 4.01.3 minutes for nine years and some people wondered if the sub-four-minute mile was an insurmountable obstacle for the human body. During his training, Roger used visualization to see himself running the race. He pictured himself entering the corners, varying his pace as needed, accelerating, and crossing the finish line. Just as he had visualized, Roger won the race and did it in under four minutes. Speaking in 2002, he said, "All sporting events are more mental than physical. You have to train the physical aspect for years . . . but the real question is whether the brain can be allowed to do its bit without being interfered with by psychological factors . . . it must be positive."

Synthetic experiences already have an impact on your life. Make sure they are working for you, instead of against you. *Always picture things turning out the way you want them to turn out.*

CHAPTER 8: Take the Lid Off

Whatever the mind can conceive and believe, the mind can achieve.
—Napoleon Hill

Hopefully, after reading the previous chapters, you are starting to realize the unlimited potential you possess. Now is the time to put it all together, and to show how the simple act of goal-setting can help bring your dreams to reality.

In 2007, Dr. Gail Matthews, a clinical psychologist at Dominican University of California, recruited participants, ranging in age from 23 to 72, from a variety of businesses, organizations, and networking groups across the world. They were divided into five groups, each one doing a more detailed business plan than the last.

Groups 1 through 5, had to think in detail about goals they wanted to accomplish over the next four weeks.
Groups 2 through 5 were required to also write down their goals.
Groups 3 through 5 then needed to formulate written commitments along with their goals.
Groups 4 and 5 had to share those commitments with a friend and finally Group 5 had to finish off by sending a weekly progress report to the friend.

At the end of the study, Groups 2 through 5 averaged higher achievement than Group 1. Group 5 participants accomplished 76 percent of their goals.

If goal-setting creates such powerful results in our lives, why doesn't everyone do it?
Because:

- It takes initiative to discover what you want
- Most people don't know how to set goals properly
- Many people doubt their abilities or are fearful of the disappointment that could result if they don't succeed
- It's hard to see ourselves outside of our current boundaries

The following story helps to illustrate that concept. It was discovered in a large aquarium, filled with sharks and other fish, that the glass wall dividing the sharks from the fish was cracked and needed to be repaired. After much thought, it was determined that they couldn't just take the divider out and repair it because the sharks would then have access to attack and kill the other helpless fish. Engineers had devised a costly method for solving the problem and they were about to proceed when a man who understood sharks explained to them that they could indeed remove the glass divider without any harm to the other fish. Once the divider was removed they observed the sharks as they would swim to the place where the divider was usually positioned and then quickly swim away. They had now realized that when the aquarium was first built, the sharks would swim into the glass divider time after time, until finally they accepted that they couldn't swim through it; so they never swam past that point again.

Just like these sharks, we all have what I like to refer to as an imaginary lid; it is what holds us back and why we create self-imposed boundaries and limitations. It keeps us within our status quo and tells us that we can accomplish *this*, but we can't accomplish *that*. This lid continually keeps us at a certain level in life. If someone is accustomed to getting Cs in school, they may unknowingly start to sabotage and not work as hard if their grades begin to climb. If their grades start to decline, they will begin working harder to bring the grade back to a C. People do the same thing with their careers, their finances and their relationships.

Breaking free of your personal restrictions is the concept I call "**Take the Lid Off.**" When you Take the Lid Off you are allowing yourself the ability to achieve greater things but it also means pushing yourself and putting yourself into new and unfamiliar situations.

Think about how everyone has certain people that they are at ease being around and things they are comfortable doing. Whenever we get around new people or do new things, we quickly find ourselves out of our comfort zone. We leave unconscious thinking and move to conscious thinking, and then our logic tells us that we're more likely to make mistakes and look like a fool in these new situations.

Most people go through their lives doing everything they can to stay in their comfort zone because they believe it is a less painful way to live. The paradox is that if you try to stay in your comfort zone it doesn't stay the same size; it gets smaller. As a result, you actually end up being out of your comfort zone more often. Likewise, if you purposely get out of your comfort zone, you develop more skills and your comfort zone keeps getting larger, leaving fewer opportunities in the future to be uncomfortable and ungraceful.

COMFORT ZONE

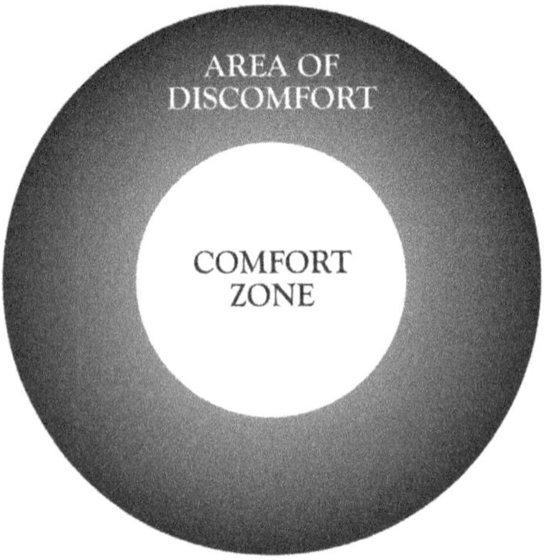

Comfort Zone includes people you are comfortable being around and activities you are comfortable doing

Get Out of Your Comfort Zone

Advantages	Disadvantages
▪ You'll grow	▪ You'll make more mistakes
▪ You'll develop talents	▪ You'll look ungraceful
▪ You'll meet more people	▪ It can be painful
▪ Your self-image will improve	▪ You'll feel out of control
▪ Your self-confidence will improve	▪ Others may be threatened

SMALL COMFORT ZONE

The harder you try to stay in your comfort zone
the smaller it gets

The smaller your comfort zone gets
the more often you will end up out of your comfort zone

LARGE COMFORT ZONE

The more you get out of your comfort zone
the larger it gets

The larger your comfort zone gets
the less often you will be FORCED out of your comfort zone

You will never be able to purposely get out of your comfort zone until you learn to stop taking yourself so seriously. Be willing to make mistakes and look clumsy. Tell your logic to stop worrying so much and just relax and have faith. The truth is, no one else cares about your mistakes because they're too busy worrying about how they look. The less you worry about your failures, the more graceful you end up being. Learn from your mistakes and then move on.

As you learn how to Take the Lid Off, it will definitely require stretching yourself outside of your normal limits.

How do you get out of your comfort zone, stretch your mind, and achieve things that you never thought possible? By moving from what I call traditional goal-setting to Take The Lid Off Goal-Setting.

Take the Lid Off Goal-Setting Theory

When we combine the Unconscious and the Conscious Mind with the Emotional and the Logical Mind, it looks like this:

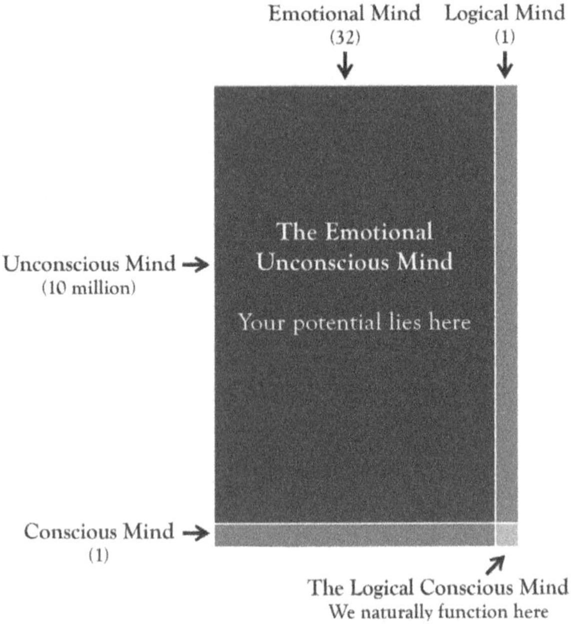

Put the two together and it's easy to see how your mind works, and how you can take advantage of its full power.

Traditional Goal-Setting

Traditional goal-setting taps into the power of your unconscious mind, but because the goal is realistic, the logical part of your mind is used instead of the emotional part.

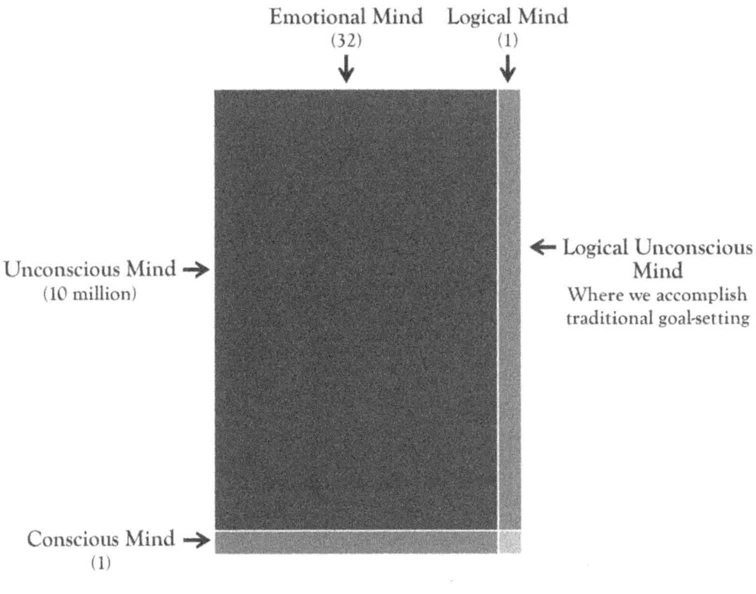

Rules for traditional goal-setting:

- Determine your goal and write it down
- Be realistic
- Be specific
- Give it a deadline

Traditional goal-setting is the standard method of goal-setting and I recommend using it to achieve the day-to-day tasks that are required of you. I also strongly suggest using it to set goals for the next 12 months as well as the next 3 years. However, traditional goal-setting only taps into the areas in which you already have confidence. It doesn't require getting out of your comfort zone; it only requires stretching it. Traditional goal-setting is your bread-and-butter and helps to improve your life. While you should make it a regular part of your routine, you should also be aware that this type of goal-setting will only take you so far.

Take the Lid Off Goal-Setting

Take the Lid Off goal-setting taps into the power of both your Emotional Mind and your Unconscious Mind.

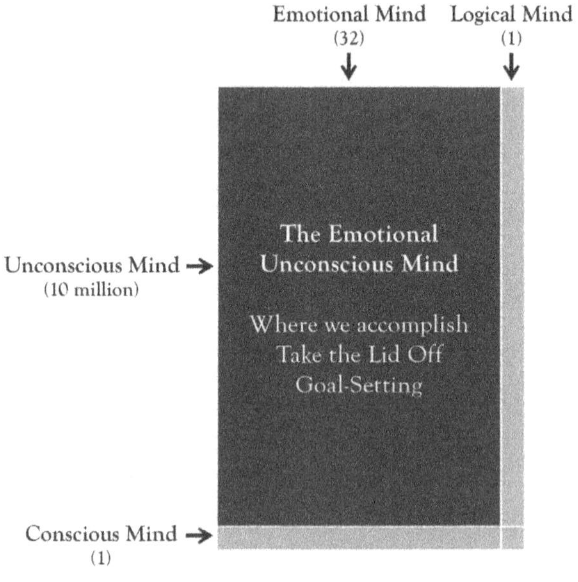

Take the Lid Off goal-setting:

- Ties into your individual genius
- Triggers your imagination
- Taps into the intelligence in space
- Reprograms your self-image
- Helps fulfill your purpose in life

Your Emotional Unconscious Mind has a vast amount of brain power just waiting to be tapped. The following concept will teach you how to access that power.

Take The Lid Off Goal-Setting starts with creating your Dream List. Imagine that you've found Aladdin's lamp and you've been given 10 wishes. Make a list of 10 things you want to have happen to you.

- Word your list as if it has already happened
- Don't be realistic
- Don't give it a deadline
- Don't share your list
- Don't worry about how it will happen

Read your list when you first get up and just before going to bed. This serves two purposes: the first will help bring your self-image and your goal closer together. The second will help your goal-seeking device and the Law of Attraction do what they do best—find ways to bring your dreams closer to you.

Examples for your Dream List:
I have a book on The New York Times *bestseller list.*
I'm Vice President of my company.

I play running back for the Pittsburg Steelers.

I am a famous artist.

I live in a beautiful new home with an indoor swimming pool.

I completed the New York City Marathon.

I weigh ________

I earn $ ________

I have saved $ ________

I have a degree in ________

Your Dream List needs to be what is important to you. If you're not sure what to put on it you can try picturing yourself five or ten years from now. What would your ideal life look like?

Also, make the format of your Dream List applicable to you. The example above is how I prefer to write my Dream List, but I know of people who use a Vision Board (a collection of pictures or images that acts as a representation of your goal), or a combination of words and pictures. Some like to have their Dream List posted in different areas of the house or they put reminder objects in strategic places.

A great example of this comes from the actor Jim Carrey. In 1987, when Carrey was struggling to make it as a comic in Los Angeles and dreaming of becoming a top-paid actor, he wrote himself a check for $10 million, marking it "for acting services rendered," and dating it Thanksgiving, 1995. For years he carried that check in his wallet as a reminder of what he eventually wanted to achieve. In 1994 he was offered $10 million to star in the movie *Dumb & Dumber* and by 1995 his asking price was $20 million a picture.

If you feel confident about achieving the items on your Dream List, you may not have set your goals high enough. If you did it correctly, you will have a hard time seeing how you will achieve many of them. That's okay—just let the ideas in. Traditional goal-setting is realistic but your Dream List is designed to help you Take the Lid Off and stretch yourself.

Don't give yourself a deadline because it will cause you to hold back. Dream as big as your imagination will allow without giving your logical mind a chance to throw cold water on your ideas. Besides, your self-image isn't ready yet to help you achieve such a large goal.

Don't feel that you have to share your list. You are less likely to really stretch out there for fear that others might think your goals are too high. Just because they can't see it doesn't mean you can't. So if you choose to share your goals, make sure it is with individuals you can trust to be supportive.

Don't worry about how you will accomplish the things on your list. It is the job of your goal-seeking device to figure that out.

Remind yourself that you don't *have* to achieve the things on your list. If your mind thinks it has to accomplish something, it automatically shifts from your emotional unconscious mind to your logical conscious mind. You must want something without *having* to *have* it.

Word your list as if it has already happened because your unconscious mind has a tendency to believe what it is told.

It is important to read your list when you first get up in the morning. Reading your list in the morning helps remind you what your goals are as you begin your day. Then read your list again just prior to going to sleep. This way your mind is pondering it as you drift off to sleep. The easiest way for me to remember to read my list is to put a copy of it on my bathroom mirror. Find a place that works the best for you.

Reading your list regularly causes structural tension. Structural tension happens when the mind wants to close the gap between reality and your goal. The more often you read the list and the more emotions you feel as you do it; the more structural tension you create. Think of it as someone nagging you to complete a task. Eventually you will want to get your mind off your back by completing the goal.

Here are a couple of examples of creating structural tension. My granddaughter once wrote an affirmation and put it on her mirror. It simply said: "I have a new friend." By placing it on her mirror, she reminded herself daily about her desire. Within two months a new girl moved to town and they have been good friends ever since.

Our administrative assistant Joanne, before she came to work for us, had put an affirmation on the door of her bathroom cabinet which stated, "I have a job that I love doing, in a nice office, with co-workers I enjoy being around, by December 9." By putting it in a strategic spot, she ensured that she read it multiple times each day. When we started the hiring process, we were planning to start our new employee January 2; but because a few situations in the office changed, we ended up having Joanne start December 9. We didn't find out about her note on the cabinet door until after we hired her.

Sometimes seeing things every day will cause it to happen fairly quickly, or like in Joanne's story—exactly when you want it to. But if your goals fail to occur when you thought they would, don't try to force them, just let them come about naturally. Keep working on your habits and skills, as well as reading your list, and give your self-image a chance to catch up.

Another aspect to consider when setting goals is coming to grips with what your goals will do to your life. Would becoming president of your company require you to spend more time away from your family than you are willing to spend? Make sure your goals line up with what you want out of life.

As you read your list, you will intuitively find yourself gaining the habits, skills, and education you will need to bring your dreams to reality. Remember to keep a realistic view of life. If you are a sophomore in high school, and you have on your list: "I own my own construction business," don't drop out of school in order to forge ahead with your goal. Stay in school, and take advantage of the opportunity to prepare yourself so you will be ready when the proper time comes. It takes a wise person to keep their feet firmly planted on solid ground while reaching for the stars.

Your self-image determines your reality today.
Your imagination determines your reality for tomorrow.

After Dayle and I went broke in our motorcycle and snowmobile business, we moved into a humble rundown home out in the country. I had the goal of someday living in a beautiful home down a lane, so I put that on my dream list. At the time, my beautiful home seemed like a wish that would never become a reality.

It took 13 years to pay off all of our debts and finally we were ready to buy our dream home. We went around the community with several real estate agents looking for the perfect home. Every time we pulled up to a house I would say, "It's beautiful, but it's not down a lane." Finally out of frustration a real estate agent asked, "What's the big deal about being down a lane?" I explained to him that every morning and every night for 13 years I told myself, "We live in a beautiful home down a lane. It's got to be down a lane!"

We weren't able to find the perfect home, so we designed and built our own beautiful home—down a lane.

Over time you will find that the items on your dream list become less of a dream and more of a reality. When this starts happening, take that dream and turn it into a goal—and begin actively working towards its achievement. Eventually you will achieve your goal and when you do, take that dream off of your dream list and replace it with a new one. When I first started making my list, things took a long time to happen, but as my self-image improved, they began to happen more quickly.

People have said to me, "Carol, it's almost spooky. Over the years I've watched you put things on your list and magically they all just seem to happen." I'll admit that at times it has felt spooky for me as well. When all of the steps are in place it feels like I am being carried toward my goals by some unseen force.

Achieving our goals creates a feeling of satisfaction that enhances our lives, but if we are not careful it can cause the opposite reaction. We've all heard the expression: "Shoot for the moon and if you miss, you will at least hit the stars." This is great as long as you are satisfied with reaching the stars. If you focus on the fact that you missed hitting the moon, you will be unhappy no matter how far you went.

I've never been able to meet all of my goals all the time, but it doesn't bother me. I have developed the habit of focusing on what I did accomplish instead of what I think I should have accomplished.

Always remember that when you set goals that require you to take the lid off, you are often going to end up with a gap between your goal and your accomplishment. So, if you are in the habit of only measuring the distance between your achievement and your goal, instead of the fact that you at least made it to a certain level, you will be unhappy. You would be measuring potential achievement instead of your actual achievement. Learn to measure what you actually achieve and don't focus on what you don't.

Potential Achievement and Actual Achievement

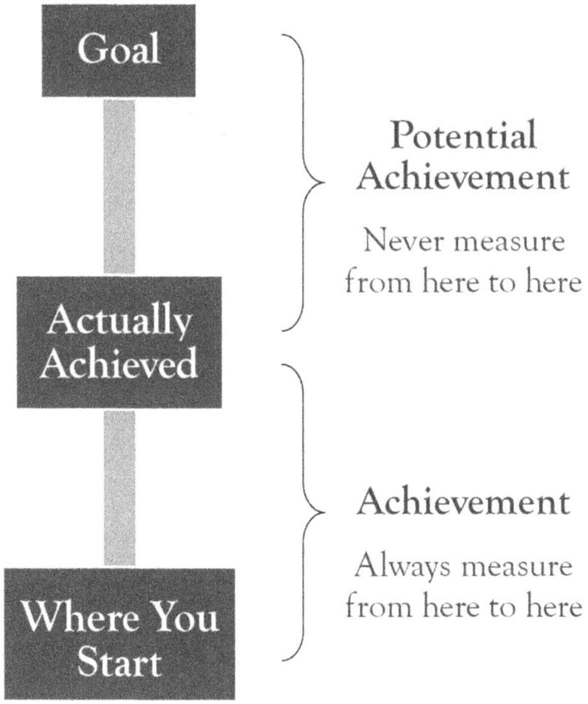

Set your goals high . . . but celebrate your small victories.

It's difficult to express the importance of goal-setting because it is such a simple thing. Yet that small act of setting a goal is the first step on your journey to realizing your unlimited potential.

You have a limited number of years to determine what impact your life will have on the world around you. At your funeral people will gather to celebrate your life and recap your journey. If you could write the script for the rest of your life, what would it be?

CHAPTER 9: Buy the Ticket

> *Unless commitment is made, there are only promises and hope—but no plans.*
>
> —Peter F. Drucker

Imagine that it has always been your dream to go to Hawaii. One evening you and your spouse are talking about your upcoming vacation and you decide this may be the year to go. You check your finances to make sure that you can afford it. You check with your parents to see if they can watch your children. Then, when you officially decide to do it, you *buy the ticket*. Once you buy the ticket, nothing gets in your way of going. Why? Simply because everything else gets scheduled around it.

After you have bought the ticket, you still have work to do, but you no longer wonder if going to Hawaii will be a reality.

Your final step is to go to the airport and get on the airplane. Once you get on board, the airplane will actually take you to Hawaii.

The same concept applies when it comes to setting goals. The moment you "Buy the Ticket," something amazing happens. Almost magically, your goal-seeking device and the law of attraction ensure that people come into your life and things happen for your benefit.

You could picture it being similar to a missile honing in on its target. The missile's guidance system sees the object but it's the warhead that "locks on" to its target. Buying the ticket is like locking the warhead on the target. Your mind can sense the slightest hesitation, so if you falter, your internal warhead won't lock on to the target. Only if you are 100 percent committed to your goal does your goal-seeking device give the work order to complete the job.

When I first went to work for New York Life, I made my dream list. One of the items on my list was: "I'm a Chairman's Council Agent." This meant that I would be in the top three percent of the company sales force. At first I couldn't comprehend being able to accomplish this goal, but it went on my list anyway. From then on I read my list every morning and every night.

Thirteen years later I decided that it was time to buy the ticket to become a Chairman's Council Agent. I called my manager in Salt Lake City and told him about my plans. At the next managers meeting he told the management team. The office manager quickly responded with, "She's all talk, she will never do it." My friend Jerry was in the meeting, and that negative comment made him mad. In my defense Jerry said, "She will too make it; in fact I'll bet you a steak dinner she does." Jerry left the meeting and called to tell me what had happened. He ended the conversation with the directive, "Carol, you have got to make Chairman's Council." I confidently said, "You can count on me, I'll do it."

About the same time my husband Dayle decided that he was going to run for sheriff of our county. I jokingly said, "You can't run for sheriff because I'm going to make Chairman's Council." Dayle threw his hat in the ring anyway and started campaigning for the position. I worked hard each day on my goal, then at night and on weekends I would help Dayle with his campaign.

In March the company sent me to Reno, Nevada to speak to the agents and help motivate them to put in the final push to reach their goals. At the end of my talk I told them about my goal to make Chairman's Council and said that I would write to them in July to let them know I made it.

Near the end of the sheriff's race we took a poll to see how Dayle was doing, the results indicated that he was losing the race. What a dilemma! Do I help Dayle with his election or do I keep my own commitment? I knew what the right answer was and so I quit selling for the month and turned my office into campaign headquarters. We brought volunteers into the office to make phone calls; and I went out campaigning full time with Dayle, knocking on doors and talking to people.

Each time my manager called to see how I was doing, I would say, "I've got it handled; I'm still going to make Chairman's Council." Then I would hang up the phone and go back out campaigning. The night of the election was exciting as we sat around the commissioners' office waiting for the results. Dayle won the election by 98 votes.

Running a political campaign was one of the most emotionally exhausting things I had ever done, so the last thing I wanted to do the next morning was go back to work on my own goal. I only had one month left to accomplish a goal that by now was way beyond anything I could comprehend. I thought about writing a letter to the agents in Reno explaining that sometimes when you buy the ticket your priorities change and you can't reach your goal. But then I thought about the office manager who had bet against me. It was just enough to remind me that I had bought the ticket and so I went back to work. It wasn't easy, but I made Chairman's Council.

I have found that one of the keys to buying the ticket is to set goals that you feel a great deal of passion for. When we lack the passion to achieve a goal, we also lack the motivation to do the hard work it will take. Remember the 32 to 1 Rule; the extra emotion that was added when my office manager bet against me was what I needed to help me stay committed to make Chairman's Council.

Cami and I had been working on this book for 10 years; we always wanted to get it written and published. It wasn't until a friend, Darren, encouraged us to commit to reporting our progress to him every week that we officially "bought the ticket" to get it done. We began reporting to him in March, and by September 1 it was finished and ready to go to the publishers.

We witnessed first-hand the goal-seeking device kicking in to help us accomplish this goal. One of our biggest road blocks to getting the book published was that I am not a trained writer.

Even though Cami has a lot of talent in putting the finishing touch on things, we both found that we were too close to the concepts and the book to be objective. We needed someone from the outside to help fine-tune the book. In stepped our administrative assistant Joanne. We had only hired her a few months earlier and little did we know back then that she had a natural instinct and ability to understand the laws we were teaching. Having her help critique and edit the book was exactly what we needed to get the project completed.

I am a firm believer that once you buy the ticket your goal-seeking device forges ahead and figures out the best path to your goal to complete it. Along with that help from your goal-seeking device, the law of attraction steps in to bring you the added talent you need to fill the gaps where your ability to achieve your goal is inadequate. The Law of Attraction will also open the doors to opportunities that were not available to you until you made the commitment and had the faith that your goal would become reality. I should know; I've experienced it over and over again and it is definitely something magical and unexplainable that happens.

The most amazing buy-the-ticket experience that has ever happened to me was when I decided to lead New York Life in sales. New York Life refers to this as being "Council President"—the top agent in a given year.

For seven years I had the statement: "I'm New York Life's Council President" on my Dream List. It was 1998 and, since I had been speaking to audiences all over the country teaching them how to tap into the power of their minds to reach their goals, I decided it was time to buy the ticket for my own dream.

To be honest, it was scary. I was now putting everything on the line in order to prove that the laws I had been teaching really worked.

The last three years my business had taken quantum leaps. I had gone from being 47th to 27th and then 14th in the company. But being the top agent would require doing almost three times as much as I had ever done before. I must have been crazy to think that I could make that kind of leap in just one year. But I had a plan. I kept track of everything I did, so I knew how many days I had to work, how many phone calls I needed to make, and, most importantly, what kind of attitude I would have to maintain to pull it off.

I knew that I would be competing with advisors from the big cities who worked with movie stars and large corporations. I, on the other hand, lived in a small town of 11,000 people and mostly worked with farmers, small business owners, and people employed at the Atomic Energy Commission an hour away. Although many of my clients were financially successful, I had not worked with anyone of "movie star" financial caliber.

Three months before the contest started I began telling everyone I knew about my goal. While I was in London at a meeting for the top agents, I told Sy Sternberg, CEO of New York Life, other board members, and some of my fellow top producers that I was going to make it.

Nobody in our industry had ever done this before. Usually an agent would already have it "in the bag" before forging ahead and they certainly didn't publicly announce their intentions ahead of time. I always pictured it being like Babe Ruth when he pointed to the stands, supposedly indicating where he was going to hit his next homerun.

Before I could make my "run for the roses," as it was called, I knew I would have to tell my parents. Through the years I had never really talked to them about how things were going with my career, so it would have been a real shock for them if I was suddenly New York Life's top sales agent. From the time I was young I had a sense that my parents thought that it was wrong to strive for financial success, especially for a woman, and especially for one of their own daughters. It was this thinking that had deeply programmed the fear of success into my original self-image. I knew they would be more concerned than excited for me. I took a deep breath and called my 90-year-old dad to break the news. It was at that moment that I realized I wasn't just sharing a dream, I was actually warning him about an event that I already knew would occur. I had seen it in my mind so vividly that I had no doubt what the results would be. After I told him, he paused and asked, "Doesn't New York Life have a lot of agents?" "About 10,000," I answered. There was another very long pause. He then said, "Carol, don't give up your values." I promised him I wouldn't.

You may think that everything I touched that year turned to gold, but I ran into many obstacles and had more things go wrong than you can ever imagine.

As we neared the end of the contest it appeared that there were only two of us still in the running. Joe, an agent from St. Louis, had led the whole year, but I had just squeaked by and taken the lead. New York Life posted the results daily on the internet so everyone in the company could track our progress.

Phone calls and e-mails were flooding our office from people I had never even met cheering me on. During the final week of the contest our local floral shop delivered a dozen roses to my office. They were from Joe with a card saying, "It's time to stop and smell the roses." I knew I had won.

CHAPTER 10: Your Power to Choose

To live is to choose. But to choose well, you must know who you are, what you stand for, where you want to go and why you want to get there.
—Kofi Annan

Every time you feel a strong emotion, your brain releases a chemical. When a thought is positive, kind or happy, a chemical is released that helps make your body feel good. When a thought is negative, angry or resentful, a chemical is released that makes you feel bad. This creates a chain reaction; the chemicals that are released will influence the next thoughts, and those thoughts then determine what chemicals the brain will release. This cycle keeps going until you make a conscious effort to change the direction of your thoughts.

If you have just been faced with a challenging situation, such as being fired, your first thought might be, "It will be hard to find a new job." From there your next thought could be "We may lose our home," which leads into, "This could ruin our credit," or "Our friends may think I did something wrong that caused me to get fired." Your thoughts will continue spiraling downward until you purposely turn them around. Stop what you are doing and think a more healthy thought. Tell yourself, "This could be a blessing in disguise because I have always wanted to start my own business," which may then lead into, "Our family is strong and we can handle this." During difficult times it becomes even more important to make a conscious effort to shift your thinking back to positive.

Benjamin Libet of the University of California experimented with how our brains function when it comes to our power to choose. Each time we have an impulse to do, think, or say something, we have two-tenths of second to veto the impulse. When you have the impulse to have a negative thought, you have two-tenths of second to change that thought to a more productive one. The results of his studies teach us that we are accountable for our spur-of-the moment decisions. It is these small day-to-day decisions that make up the texture of our lives. We are not always going to be faced with extreme, challenging situations that require a large amount of effort to remain positive, but everyday life is made up of little challenges that require us to make many small choices each day. These determine the quality of your life, whether it's being happy, successful, etc.

Make the Best of Day-to-Day Decisions

An old Jewish folktale tells of a man who lived in a small house with his wife, numerous children and grandchildren, his parents, and his in-laws. The noise and clutter drove him to distraction, until one day he finally went to his rabbi asking for advice.

The rabbi told him that he must bring the chickens into his house. The man was puzzled, but he knew the rabbi was very wise so he went home and placed all the chickens inside his home. The constant clucking and flapping only made matters worse and the man returned to the rabbi asking what he could do to relieve the chaos. The rabbi said he must now bring the sheep and the goats into the house. Again, he did as the rabbi said, but the chickens laid eggs in the beds, the sheep baa'd constantly, the goats ate anything they found, and the whole place smelled like a barnyard. The poor man was overwhelmed and declared to the rabbi that he had done all that was asked of him but that things were worse than ever.

This time the rabbi told him to return the chickens to the coop, and the goats and sheep to the fields. As he did so, his wife and family cleaned and tidied all of the rooms. When the work was done, they all agreed that the space and the serenity within the little house made it the most comfortable home in the village. The man was, at last, content.

So many times we choose to focus on what is wrong in our lives and that leads us to be unhappy with our current circumstances. It is these day-to-day decisions, whether you see things as a positive or negative, that will start to influence your thoughts.

If you allow negative thoughts to continue, you will find that not only do you focus on current circumstances, but you will soon start to think about past injustices as well, causing you to feel miserable even if everything around you is wonderful. The result is that far too much energy is spent on being offended instead of on being happy.

In his short story, *The Piece of String*[14], French writer Guy de Maupassant tells of a peasant named Maître Hauchecome who came to the local village on market day. While walking toward the public square, his eye caught sight of a piece of string lying on the ground. He picked up the small piece of string and put it in his pocket. Unbeknownst to him, his actions were observed by the village harness maker, with whom he had previously had a dispute.

Later in the day the loss of a purse was reported. Hauchecome was questioned because of an accusation from the harness maker. He was then taken before the mayor, to whom he protested his innocence, showing it was only a piece of string that he had picked up. But he was not believed and was laughed at.

The next day the purse was found and Hauchecome was absolved of any wrongdoing. But, resentful of the indignity he had suffered because of false accusation from the harness maker, he became embittered and would not let the matter die. Unwilling to forgive and forget, he thought and talked of little else. Everywhere he went, everyone he met had to be told of the injustice. By day and by night he brooded over it. Obsessed with his grievance, he wasted away and died. In the delirium of the death struggles, he repeatedly murmured, "A piece of string, a piece of string—look—here it is, M'sieu Mayor."

The quality of our lives depends on whether we focus on positive or negative memories from the past and then how we use them to envision our future. Focusing on happy, upbeat memories to produce an optimistic vision of the future is a positive use of our imagination. Conversely, when we focus on memories of sadness or anger, worry becomes a negative product of the misuse of our imagination

Master Your Response to Negative Situations

We are all going to have negative thoughts. But they can't harm us if they are quickly discarded as soon as they come into our mind. Picture yourself sitting around a campfire with embers from the fire flying into the air. If a hot ember lands on your clothing, it won't do any damage if you quickly brush it off. However, if it stays on your clothes it will start to burn a hole. It works the same way with negative thoughts. When they come into your mind, quickly brush them away and they won't do any harm. Develop the habit of monitoring your thoughts. When they are negative, simply make the conscious effort to shift them to positive. Eventually you will do it automatically and effortlessly.

Even if you follow the laws and habits that have been outlined in the previous chapter, it will not eliminate failure from being a part of your life. Challenges can come from many sources such as acts of nature as well as the fact that others have their ability to choose their thoughts and actions; which means that their choices can impact your life as well. Even though you have the power to choose, you still only have total control over two things: the thoughts *you* think and the actions *you* take.

Even if we could magically control our lives so that nothing bad ever happened to us, it wouldn't be a good thing. Consider this: how would you know what it feels like to be happy, if you have never experienced sorrow? None of us enjoy failing or dealing with challenging situations, but without those experiences we would never fully develop our emotional mind. It's the price we pay to reach our full potential.

Pickles are an interesting example that can teach us a great deal about this process. A dill pickle is a cucumber that has been transformed by being immersed in harsh salt brine for a certain period of time. During the curing process, the cucumber gradually takes on a new appearance and then eventually a new taste. It doesn't work to occasionally dip the cucumber into the brine or to casually sprinkle it with salt; this will not produce the necessary transformation. There are no shortcuts in creating a pickle.

It is the same for each of us. The trials and disappointments of life help us gradually transform and take on the qualities we would not be able to acquire on our own. When we are experiencing difficult times, we are also more open and teachable than at any other time; thus causing paradigm shifts and our self-image to realign, all of which would be impossible to do on our own. Look at it this way; some of life's challenging events are more about discovering our innate self-worth than about our ability to accomplish great feats.

Failure is just as important to our growth and development as success; both are required for us to fully develop emotionally. Failure makes us teachable and helps build our character, while success builds our confidence and in some cases even goes on to serve humanity.

Overcome Barriers to Success

Be aware that there will be times when you lose your confidence. When this happens, you must work toward new goals because one way to regain your confidence is by feeling the achievement that comes with reaching a goal.

Whether you have just lost your job, broken up with a loved one or made a major mistake, this can be the perfect time to turn things around. This is your time of greatest potential because it is during these times that your senses are the most alive and ready to learn. If you persevere, you could be on the verge of a tremendous breakthrough. Maybe you were supposed to make a one-hundred-and-eighty-degree turn in your life. If things are going smoothly, do you think you would be willing to make drastic changes? It's usually not until our lives are already turned upside down that we decide, "I have nothing to lose."

Another one of the greatest obstacles for achieving our desires is our fear of failure. Nobody likes to fail, but it is a natural part of life. In order to forge ahead in spite of our setbacks, we must learn to look at failure in a different light. We often think that as we experience greater success, we will somehow break through the clouds and reach a point where failure is no longer part of our existence. In reality, failure compounds itself as you stretch to greater heights. At this point you must learn how to use your failures as stepping stones instead of stumbling blocks to reach your goals.

> *It's not the critic who counts; not the man who points out how the strong man stumbles or where the doer of deeds could have done them better.*

> *The credit belongs to the man who is actually in the arena, whose face is marred by dust and sweat and blood; who strives valiantly; who errs, who comes short again and again; who knows the great enthusiasms—the great devotions; who, when he succeeds knows the triumph of high achievement; and who, if he fails, at least fails while daring greatly so that his place shall never be with those cold and timid souls who know neither victory nor defeat.*
>
> —THEODORE ROOSEVELT

Far too often we let our fears stop us. We dream of great things, and then we question our ability to pull it off by reminding ourselves how foolish we were to even consider accomplishing such a feat in the first place. So we give up. When you have great dreams, it is your soul trying to help you recognize your potential and encourage you to lead a happy and fulfilling life. Dreams are placed in your heart for a reason; don't ignore them.

Success is many things to different people. My favorite definition is: success is the progressive realization of a worthwhile goal. You may have a desire to become a better person, improve your relationships with your loved ones or create a satisfying career. As you measure your success, keep in mind that success is not the end result; success is the process. In other words, success is a journey, not the destination. As long as you are moving toward your goal, you are succeeding.

George Frideric Handel is best known for his composition of *Messiah* and its famous movement, the "Hallelujah Chorus." However, his life had plenty of opposition as well. He was a musical child prodigy, and by the time he was 40 he was a celebrated composer. Even with all of his fame, his audiences were unpredictable and he struggled as he tried to compete with the other opera companies in London. Soon his defeats were more common than his successes. He drove himself relentlessly until finally his health began to fail. His failures were so profound that it appeared he might end up in debtor's prison. In 1741, at the age of 56, he considered leaving England after the failure of his latest opera.

That summer, a wealthy friend, Charles Jennens, gave Handel a libretto based on the life of Christ. In the remarkably short time of 24 days Handel composed all 260 pages of the first draft. *Messiah* premiered April 13, 1742, in Dublin as a charitable benefit for the Society for Relieving Prisoners, the Charitable Infirmary, and Mercer's Hospital. The concert raised 400 pounds, with 127 pounds going to each of the three charities. He personally conducted more than thirty performances of Messiah and many of these concerts were to provide benefits for charities. One biographer stated, "Messiah has fed the hungry, clothed the naked, and fostered the orphan. . . more than any other single musical production in this or any country."[15]

We all have times when we doubt ourselves. The key is to develop the habit of forging ahead in spite of your fears because even though it may not feel like it at the time, you are actually already succeeding if you are working toward your dream.

Never Give Up

When we read about unusual success we have a tendency to think these people are different from us. The only thing different is that successful people have learned how to tap into the power of the laws of success. When we work to align ourselves so that our self-image matches our goals, and then we develop the habits of success, we have amazing potential as well.

But success seldom happens overnight. Many people try the principles of success for awhile and then give up, stating that the principles just don't work for them. The bamboo plant teaches us that not everything happens quickly. As the rhizomes develop, little happens above ground for the first few years while the system is established. However, when everything is ready, during an eight-week period, the stems can grow 70 feet.

There are countless stories about great men and women who never gave up on their dreams:

- In 1878, Thomas Edison boldly announced to the world that he would invent an inexpensive, long-lasting electric light. It took 14 months, and his lab conducted over 1,200 different experiments before he finally demonstrated his first carbon-filament incandescent light bulb on October 21, 1879.
- When Bell Telephone was struggling to get started, its owners offered all their patents to Western Union for $100,000. The offer was rejected.
- After Harrison Ford's first movie performance as an actor, the studio vice president called him into his office and dismissed him with, "You ain't got it, kid, you ain't got it . . . now get out of here."
- Walt Disney once went bankrupt and the proposed Disneyland park was rejected by the City of Burbank because city officials did not want "the carny atmosphere."

- Michael Jordan failed to make the varsity team in his sophomore year of high school.
- Tom Landry, Chuck Noll, Bill Walsh and Jimmy Johnson accounted for 11 out of 23 Super Bowl victories from 1972 to 1994. They also share the distinction of having some of the worst records of first-season head coaches in NFL history.

Abraham Lincoln experienced many failures in his life; and is a great example of persistence. The following is a list of some of his accomplishments and publicly known defeats. How many of us would have the tenacity to experience that many failures without giving up?

Age 22	Lost his job
Age 23	Defeated for State Legislature
Age 24	Failed in business
Age 25	Elected to Illinois State Legislature
Age 26	His sweetheart died
Age 27	Suffered severe depression
Age 34	Defeated for nomination for Congress
Age 37	Elected to Congress
Age 46	Defeated for U.S. Senate
Age 47	Defeated for nomination for Vice President
Age 49	Failed to win a seat in the U.S. Senate
Age 51	Elected President of the United States

The Gettysburg Address delivered by Abraham Lincoln in 1863 has come to be regarded as one of the best speeches in American history and yet President Lincoln was not the featured speaker that day. That honor went to Edward Everett, a noted orator from Massachusetts. The President had been invited to attend the National Cemetery's dedication ceremony at the last minute with the expectation that he would be too busy to attend. The organizers were surprised when he accepted the invitation. An estimated fifteen thousand people crowded around the speakers' platform to hear Edward Everett. With his ability to enthrall audiences, he kept them spellbound for nearly two hours. Lincoln then rose and delivered his address in less than two minutes. There was little reaction from the audience, probably because they were confused by the brevity of his speech. Seeing the audience's reaction to his speech, he said to his bodyguard, Marshal Lamon, "Lamon, that speech won't scour. It is a flat failure." The following day Everett wrote the President saying: "I should be glad if I could flatter myself that I came as near to the central idea of the occasion in two hours as you did in two minutes." As the words Lincoln spoke that day were spread by the newspapers, the public concurred that it was indeed one of the best speeches in American history.

As you can see from Abraham Lincoln's address, even our successes may appear to be failures at first. Even some of our successes may not be recognized in our lifetime. Van Gogh is known to have sold only one painting, *The Red Vineyard at Arles*, during his life and it was sold to the sister of one of his friends for 400 francs (approximately $1,500 in today's money). This didn't stop him from completing over 800 paintings that today are considered some of the most influential and coveted pieces of art.

Sometimes we simply choose to live a life of mediocrity because of our fear of criticism from others. Many dreams have been crushed on the rocks of other's harsh words.

We're all familiar with the Wright Brothers and how they invented the first successful manned airplane; but you may not be familiar with the story of Samuel Langley.

Langley, the respected head of the prestigious Smithsonian Institution, was also working on a project to develop an airplane. He was able to convince the War Department to contribute $50,000 toward the project.

His first attempt at a manned heavier-than-air flight failed, and the press was tough on Langley but he persisted in his efforts. However, after the second attempt went horribly wrong, the newspapers were unforgiving of the failure, dubbing it "Langley's Folly," ridiculing the effort, and railing about the waste of taxpayers' money.

Langley was deeply disheartened by the failure and was also deeply hurt by the negative press. Hence, despite offers of private funding, he decided not to continue his quest. Thus ended Langley's sixteen years of aerial experiments.

After Langley's second failed attempt *The New York Times* stated in an editorial, "A man-carrying airplane will eventually be built, but only if mathematicians and engineers work steadily for the next one to ten million years." Nine days later on December 17, 1903, the Wright brothers stunned the world with their invention. How thankful we are for the Wright Brothers, who didn't listen to the critics and who kept pursuing their dreams despite the failures of others!

We all have dreams. But it's our persistence, determination, and power to choose that dictates what we do with them and how much we allow ourselves to achieve.

My final thoughts can be summarized perfectly in this beautiful passage by Marianne Williamson:[16]

Our deepest fear is not that we are inadequate. Our deepest fear is that we are powerful beyond measure. It is our light, not our darkness, that most frightens us. We ask ourselves, Who am I to be brilliant, gorgeous, talented, fabulous? Actually, Who are you not *to be? You are a child of God. Your playing small does not serve the world. There is nothing enlightening about shrinking so that other people won't feel unsure around you. We are all meant to shine, as children do. We were born to make manifest the glory of God that is within us. It's not just in some of us; it is in everyone and as we let our own light shine, we unconsciously give other people permission to do the same. As we are liberated from our own fear, our presence automatically liberates others.*

CONCLUSION: Unleash Your Unlimited Potential

Every human being will have a gap between their potential and where their life is today. In fact, it is impossible to completely close the gap because our potential is *unlimited*—the more we achieve, the more we become capable of even greater achievement! Once you understand your mind and learn how to incorporate the principles for tapping into its power, you can make tremendous headway towards unleashing your unlimited potential.

Take the Lid Off is a concept that allows you to be able to envision your unlimited potential and achieve your dreams in spite of your current circumstances. We included a review of the main concepts found in the book and outlined a strategy to help you *Take the Lid Off* in your own life.

TAKE THE LID OFF CONCEPTS

Concept #1 Your Self-Image

Your self-image is your mind's conception of the kind of person you are and what you are capable of achieving. It sets the parameters and is the determining factor that dictates your behavior and lifestyle. It is also the determining factor that decides just how much of your potential you will allow into your life. Hopefully by now, you comprehend the immense hold your self-image has on you and why changing it will require a proven strategy and hard work. The bottom line is that reprogramming your self-image means making some major lifestyle changes as you work to align your self-image with your true self.

Concept #2 Habits

You only have control over two things—your thoughts and your actions. Approximately 90 percent of what you do every day you do from habit; this means that your habits are in charge of your life. When you decide to change your habits, your self-image will also change. Vice versa; when you decide to change your self-image, your habits will change to match. As soon as you begin a new habit, good or bad, you begin the process of changing your thoughts and actions which will then reprogram your self-image. But remember, don't overwhelm yourself—only work on one habit at a time.

Concept #3 Your Individual Genius

Every human being has potential genius in at least one area. Your particular genius is tied to your purpose in life, so you will feel drawn to it. Keep in mind that it comes so naturally to you that you may not even recognize it. Once you discover your potential genius it will still require years of dedicated effort to turn it from potential to individual genius.

Concept #4 Your Goal-Seeking Device

Your goal-seeking device always needs a goal to work towards and when you do not set goals, you are wasting its amazing power. Once a goal is set, your RAS and your unlimited database go to work filtering information for you and using an infinite awareness to hunt for solutions and ideas that haven't occurred to you before. Set one goal at a time to avoid confusing your RAS about which one to focus on.

Concept #5 The 32 to 1 Rule

Your emotional mind carries a greater influence on you and your decisions than your logical mind does. Your mind wants to experience pleasure and avoid pain. Since the majority of your decisions are determined by your emotions, you will find yourself making decisions that make you feel good. That's why following through on well-intentioned goals is hard to do. Your logical mind knows what you should do but your emotions keep getting in the way. In order to reach your goals you must find creative ways to get your emotions on board. Habits are the first place to start because habits override your emotions. Adding passion to your goals and being accountable for your results are also ways of harnessing the power of your emotions.

Concept #6 The Law of Attraction

The Law of Attraction states that "like attracts like." More specifically, you attract into your life the results of the thoughts you dwell upon and what you feel you deserve. There is great power in your mind, and that power also extends to other people and out into the world as it attracts to you the results of your dominant thoughts. A great deal of your successes and failures will come to you as an indirect result of your thoughts.

Concept #7 Synthetic Experiences

Your mind doesn't know the difference between a real and a vividly imagined experience; therefore synthetic experiences function in your mind the same way real experiences do. Self-Affirmation, the "Act As If" principle, and Visualization are tactics that will help bridge the gap between your current self-image and your goal.

Concept #8 Your Comfort Zone

We all have a comfort zone in which we function most of the time. It includes people we enjoy being around and things we like doing. Once we get out of this comfort zone we are more likely to make mistakes and look foolish. Remember that our mind wants to experience pleasure and avoid pain, so most people do everything in their power to stay in their comfort zones. The problem is that your comfort zone never stays the same size, it either gets larger or it gets smaller. When you stay in your comfort zone it gets smaller, but the more you get out of your comfort zone, the bigger it becomes and the less you will find yourself being in areas of discomfort.

Concept #9 Take the Lid Off

Your self-image creates an imaginary lid that holds you back and causes self-imposed boundaries and limitations. It is what tells you that you can accomplish this, but you can't accomplish that. In order to unleash your unlimited potential you must take the lid off by creating your "Dream List." This means you must leave your comfort zone and allow yourself to dream big. When you take the lid off, you are functioning from within your Emotional-Unconscious Mind. This is the time to allow a new version of your self-image into your mind as you visualize the impact that accomplishing the things on your list will have on your life.

Concept #10 Buy the Ticket

The moment you are 100% committed to achieving your goal, you have just Bought the Ticket. It is at this point that you give the work order to your goal-seeking device to complete the job. It also signals to the world to bring the help you need through the Law of Attraction. One word of caution, when you Buy the Ticket everything else will need to be scheduled around your goal; so make sure it's a goal worth sacrificing for.

Concept #11 Your Power to Choose

One of the most amazing things about your mind is that it allows you to make conscious choices. We've continually talked about the power of your mind and how you can tap into your unlimited potential, but none of that would be available to you without your power to choose. You can choose which habits you want to develop and whether or not you magnify your individual genius. You can choose your thoughts and that creates the quality of your life. You also get to choose whether or not you will pursue your dreams and if you find a way to keep forging ahead in spite of the roadblocks that seem to crop up along the way. *Most importantly, you get to choose what kind of person you will become from this moment forward.*

TAKE THE LID OFF STRATEGY

STEP 1: DECIDE WHAT YOU WANT

CREATE YOUR DREAM LIST

Creating your Dream List is the key to Taking the Lid Off because it allows a new version of your self-image into your mind. It also helps you to recognize and develop your individual genius as well as to achieve your life's mission.

Make a list of 10 things you want to have happen to you; imagine your ideal life:

- Word your list as if it has already happened
- Don't be realistic
- Don't give it a deadline
- Don't share your list
- Don't worry about how it will happen
- Read your list every morning and every night

- When one thing on your list happens, replace it with another

STEP 2: PREPARE YOURSELF FOR SUCCESS

REPROGRAM YOUR SELF-IMAGE FOR SUCCESS

Decide what you want your self-image to be:

- Write a description of your desired self-image
- Meditate. Picture yourself acting exactly the way you want to act.

Develop good habits:

- Make a list of habits you want to change
- List your habits in order of their importance
- Choose the most important one to work on first
- Work on only one habit at a time, and work on it for about a month or until the change is accomplished and no longer takes effort

As you make changes, you will find habits in other areas of your life improving as well.

Always say things to yourself that you want to be true:

- You are the programmer for your self-image, which means that you are *the only one* with the power to reprogram your mind. It's what you say to yourself, and not what others say to you, that creates the programming.

Attach a positive meaning to the events that occur to you (E+R=O):

- You can't control all of the events in your life; but you can change your response—and that will change the outcome

Choose friends, books, movies, TV shows and music that have a positive impact on your self-image:

- What you consistently choose to expose yourself to, you will eventually incorporate into your life

DISCOVER AND DEVELOP YOUR INDIVIDUAL GENIUS

- Ask people who know you well, "What do you think my individual genius is"?
- Listen for compliments, they tend to reflect your genius
- What are you passionate about?
- What areas of learning come naturally to you?
- What activities rejuvenate and energize you?

STEP 3: MAKE IT HAPPEN

CHOOSE ONE GOAL TO WORK ON NOW

- Write your goal down
- It must be measurable and have a deadline
- Word your goal as if it has already happened
- Read your goal several times a day

Harness the power of your emotional mind

- Add passion to your goal
- Measure you activities and report the results to someone you admire

Buy the ticket

- Be 100% committed to achieving your goal
- This causes your goal-seeking device to give the work order to complete your goal

- Commitment is what sends the message to the world that you are ready for its help through the "Law of Attraction"

Use synthetic experiences to bridge the gap between your self-image and your goal

- Practice self-affirmations
- Employ the "act as if" principle
- Use visualization

Never give up

- You will experience many setbacks. Have faith and forge ahead
- Remember to celebrate the things you accomplish, and never beat yourself up when you fall short

When you Take the Lid Off, you are unleashing your unlimited potential to create the life of your dreams!

ENDNOTES

[1] Borrowman, Jerry and Holm, Carol. *Have You Bought The Ticket? Ideas to Inspire You to Achieve Your Ultimate Dreams!* Bruce Holmes, 2000.

[2] The concept of "self-image" is explored in the teachings of Maxwell Maltz. For full publishing details, see Ten Recommended Reads.

[3] Fox, Michael J. *Lucky Man: A Memoir*. Hyperion, 2002.

[4] Peltzer, Dave. *A Child Called "It": One Child's Courage to Survive*.

[5] From Soar With Your Strengths by D. Clifton and Paula Nelson, © 1992 by Selection Research, Inc. and Paula Nelson. Used by permission of Dell Publishing, a division of Random House, Inc.

[6] Unique Ability® is a registered trademark, protected by copyright and an integral concept of The Strategic Coach Inc. All rights reserved. Used with written permission. www.strategiccoach.com

[7] More information on this experiment can be found at www.bbc.co.uk/dna/h2g2/A1132480.3. I first learned of using colors to help people succeed from James R. Noland of the Personalysis Corporation, but the information found here is a result of much research and adaptation. Personalysis® information printed with permission of Personalysis, www.personalysis.com.

[8] Gladwell, Malcolm. *Outliers: The Story of Success*. Back Bay Books, 2010.

[9] The concept of the "goal-seeking device" is from Maxwell Maltz and his book *Psycho-Cybernetics*. For full publishing details, see Ten Recommended Reads.

[10] Gelb, Michael J. *How to Think Like Leonardo da Vinci: Seven Steps to Genius Every Day*. Dell, 2000.

[11] Abagnale, Frank. *Catch Me If You Can: The True Story of a Real Fake*. Broadway, 2000.

[12] Betttger, Frank. *How I Raised Myself from Failure to Success in Selling*. Fireside, 1992.

[13] Study conducted by Professor L. V. Clark of Wayne State University. (ref. L. V. Clark study) Essential Readings in Sport and Exercise Psychology. eds. Daniel Smith and Michael Bar-Eli. For more information on this experiment, visit (re: Matthews) http://www.dominican.edu/academics/ahss/psych/faculty/fulltime/gailmatthews/researchsummary2.pdf

[14] De Maupassant, Guy. *Une Vie: A Piece of String and Other Stories*. Thompson-Barlow Company, Inc., 1923.

[15] Messiah biographer quote.

[16] Williams, Marianne. *A Return to Love: Reflections on the Principles of "A Course in Miracles."* HarperCollins, 1992.

TEN RECOMMENDED READS

1. ***Failing Forward: Turning Mistakes Into Stepping Stones for Success*** by John C. Maxwell. Thomas Nelson, 2007.
   It's a great book about putting failure into perspective.
2. ***How to Win Friends and Influence People*** by Dale Carnegie. Pocket Books, 1958.
   Carnegie teaches the rules for developing effective people skills.
3. ***Power vs. Force: The Hidden Determinants of Human Behavior*** by David R. Hawkins, M.D., PhD. Veritas Publishing, 1995.
   According to Hawkins, our power comes from within. We each have an energy level that is either positive or negative. He teaches us how to raise our energy levels.
4. ***Psycho-Cybernetics: A New Way to Get More Living Out of Life*** by Maxwell Maltz, M.D., F.I.C.S. Pocket Books, 1989.

Cybernetics teaches us that our physical brain and nervous system make up a servo-mechanism, which operates very much like a computer or a guided missile. Maltz also teaches his theories about our self-image.

5. ***The Greatest Salesman in the World*** by Og Mandino. Frederick Fell, 1973.
   Og Mandino is a master story teller and in this book he uses ten stories set in ancient times to teach the principles of effective salesmanship.
6. ***The Richest Man in Babylon*** by George S. Clason. Infinite Ideas, 2008.
   Clason teaches us that money is plentiful for those who understand the simple laws which govern its acquisition.
7. ***The Road Less Traveled: A New Psychology of Love, Traditional Values, and Spiritual Growth*** by M. Scott Peck, M.D. Simon & Schuster, 1979.
   Peck is a psychiatrist who teaches us how to reach a higher level of self-awareness.
8. ***The 7 Habits of Highly Effective People*** by Stephen R. Covey. Free Press, 2004.
   Covey teaches us how to be effective when it comes to getting things done.
9. ***Think & Grow Rich: A Black Choice*** by Dennis Kimbro and Napoleon Hill. Fawcett, 1992.
   This book is the result of a twenty-year study of some of the most successful people in the world. Hill teaches us what he learned about what it takes to succeed.
10. ***Who Moved My Cheese?: An Amazing Way to Deal with Change in Your Work and in Your Life*** by Spencer Johnson, M.D. G. P. Putnam's Sons, 1998.

INDEX

C

D

E

F

G

H

I

J

K

L

M

S

T

U

V

W